The Life of
Adam and Eve
and Related Literature

Guides to Apocrypha and Pseudepigrapha

Series Editor
Michael A. Knibb

The Life of
ADAM and EVE
and Related Literature

Marinus de Jonge
& Johannes Tromp

Sheffield
Academic Press

Copyright © 1997 Sheffield Academic Press

Published by Sheffield Academic Press Ltd
Mansion House
19 Kingfield Road
Sheffield S11 9AS
England

Printed on acid-free paper in Great Britain
by The Cromwell Press
Melksham, Wiltshire

British Library Cataloguing in Publication Data

A catalogue record for this book is available
from the British Library

ISBN 1-85075-764-X

Contents

Preface

An introduction to the Adam literature in the series 'Guides to Apocrypha and Pseudepigrapha' has, of necessity, to be selective. Following Michael Stone in his *A History of the Literature of Adam and Eve* (1992), we distinguish between 'primary' and 'secondary' Adam literature, and we have decided to concentrate on the documents belonging to the first category. They are:

The Greek *Apocalypse of Moses*, or: the Greek *Life of Adam and Eve*

The Latin *Vita Adae et Evae*

The Slavonic *Life of Adam and Eve*

The Armenian *Penitence of Adam*

The Georgian *Book of Adam*

One or two Coptic versions, of which only few fragments exist.

In the first four chapters of this book attention will be paid to these writings, which are, in fact, different versions of one book, a *Life of Adam and Eve*. We shall focus on the contents of the documents and the relationships between them, as well as on their individual features. We shall not be able to avoid a number of (rather technical) textual and literary-historical questions. In these fields relatively little has been done recently, and clarification of a number of these issues has proved necessary before an adequate description of the constitutive elements and main themes of the different versions of the *Life of Adam and Eve* could be given.

The last chapter will be devoted to the most important of the many writings ranged by Stone under the heading 'secondary Adam Literature'. Among the many writings belonging to that category we selected the *Discourse on Abbatôn*, the *Testament of Adam*, the *Cave of Treasures*, the *Conflict of Adam and Eve with Satan* and the *Apocalypse of Adam*.

For all serious work on any problem related to the Adam literature M.E. Stone's *History* is an indispensable tool. In the Introduction to that work the author emphasizes that his primary aim was to bring together and to assess recent research in order to stimulate new work ('The purpose of the present book is not to make a new contribution to the resolution of these complex issues. It is to make a clear and integrated assessment and presentation of what is currently known about the various textual, literary and transmission historical aspects of the Adam literature' [p. viii]). In a modest way this guide wants to contribute to new solutions to questions that have not yet found satisfactory answers—at least as far as the versions of the *Life of Adam and Eve* are concerned. The authors realize, of course, that the brief indications that they can give in the present context call for a more elaborate presentation of the evidence. In due course they hope to come back to those problems in further publications.

For the work on the *Life of Adam and Eve* another tool was constantly used: *A Synopsis of the Books of Adam and Eve*, edited by Gary Anderson and Michael Stone (1994). Earlier, the authors benefitted from the discussions in the seminar on 'Early Jewish Literature and the New Testament' of the international *Studiorum Novi Testamenti Societas* that devoted its sessions in 1990–1992 to the versions of the *Life of Adam and Eve*. M.E. Stone gave us much helpful advice. J. van der Vliet assisted us in assessing the Coptic material. M.A. Knibb and H.W. Hollander read the manuscript and suggested a number of clarifications. The authors are very much obliged to all of them.

Marinus de Jonge
Johannes Tromp

Related Reading

At the end of most sections or chapters, the main relevant literature is mentioned with full titles. In the text the books and articles cited are mentioned with short titles. All titles are mentioned in full in the Select Bibliography at the end of this book.

M.E. Stone, *A History of the Literature of Adam and Eve* (SBL Early Judaism and its Literature, 3; Atlanta: Scholars Press, 1992).

G.A. Anderson and M.E. Stone, *A Synopsis of the Books of Adam and Eve* (SBL Early Judaism and its Literature, 5; Atlanta: Scholars Press, 1994).

Abbreviations

Arm.	The Armenian version of the *Life of Adam and Eve* (*Penitence of Adam*)
Copt.	The Coptic fragment(s)
Georg.	The Georgian version of the *Life of Adam and Eve* (*Book of Adam*)
GLAE	The Greek version of the *Life of Adam and Eve* (*Apocalypse of Moses*)
LAE	*Life of Adam and Eve*
LLAE	The Latin version of the *Life of Adam and Eve* (*Vita Adae et Evae*)
Slav.	The Slavonic version of the *Life of Adam and Eve*

ANT	*The Apocryphal New Testament*
CRINT	Compendia rerum iudaicarum ad Novum Testamentum
CSCO	Corpus scriptorum christianorum orientalium
EPROER	Etudes préliminaires aux religions orientales dans l'Empire Romain
HTR	*Harvard Theological Review*
HUCA	*Hebrew Union College Annual*
JJS	*Journal of Jewish Studies*
JSJ	*Journal for the Study of Judaism*
JSP	*Journal for the Study of the Pseudepigrapha*
JTS	*Journal of Theological Studies*
NS	New Series
OTP	*The Old Testament Pseudepigrapha*
SBL	Society of Biblical Literature
SBLDS	SBL Dissertation Series
SBLSP	SBL Seminar Papers
SVTP	Studia in Veteris Testamenti pseudepigrapha
VC	*Vigiliae Christianae*
VOHD	Verzeichnis der orientalischen Handschriften in Deutschland

1

THE MOST RECENT EDITIONS AND THE CONTENTS OF THE DIFFERENT VERSIONS OF THE *LIFE OF ADAM AND EVE*

The *Life of Adam and Eve*, in its various forms, presents fascinating reading. Retelling the story in Genesis 3 of Adam's and Eve's transgression of God's commandment and their expulsion from the Garden of Eden, it explores the effects of these events for humanity.

In the Greek version, the earliest of the five in our opinion, Adam looks back only briefly on what happened in the Garden, but Eve tells the story at some length, highlighting the part played by the serpent as a tool of Satan. Very important is what follows: the elaborate description of Adam's death, his assumption to Paradise in the third heaven, and his being buried together with his son Abel—finally followed by the burial of Eve. There is hope for human beings on this earth. God is full of grace; the survival of Adam in the heavenly Paradise, as well as his future resurrection, are as much a paradigm for humanity as his transgression, condemnation and death.

The Greek *Life* selected a number of existing traditions concerning Adam and Eve and incorporated them in a document with a clear message for its readers. It hints at other traditions, part of which are told in a more elaborate form in the other versions, which used additional (oral and/or written) sources beside the Greek. Each version has its own mix of traditional material, and its own purpose in telling the story. The versions taken together present a complex but interesting mosaic of reflections on the human plight, inspired by the Genesis story.

The study of the different versions of the *Life of Adam and Eve* is beset with many problems. For a long time attention was focused on the Greek and Latin versions and, to a lesser extent, also on the

Slavonic. More recently, editions of the Georgian and Armenian have become available. They form a welcome addition to the evidence, particularly because they seem to occupy a middle position between the Greek and the Latin.

On the other hand this new material now makes it necessary to sort out the relationships between no less than *five* clearly related but in many respects different documents. (The fragmentary state of the Coptic evidence does not allow us to draw any significant conclusions.) In this and the three following chapters we shall have to apply several critical methods to arrive at reliable results—and even so some can only be tentative. It is necessary to disentangle a number of knotty problems before we are able to concentrate on the meaning and message of the *Life of Adam and Eve* in its various forms.

The Most Recent Editions

The *Greek Life of Adam and Eve* (*Apocalypse of Moses*)

The writing which we designate here as the (Greek) *Life of Adam and Eve* is actually called, in most Greek manuscripts, 'The Story (diegesis) of Adam and Eve'. When C. Tischendorf published the writing in his collection of apocryphal apocalypses (*Apocalypses Apocryphae*, 1866), he called it the *Apocalypse of Moses*. This designation has since been rejected as a misnomer, although most manuscripts do assert that this writing was 'revealed to Moses when he received the tables of the Law' (compare the beginning of *Jubilees*). This phrase, however, is a claim to authority only, and the writing contains no further references to its alleged Mosaic origin whatsoever. For clarity's sake, therefore, the title *Greek Life of Adam and Eve* (*GLAE*) is to be preferred.

M. Nagel's *La vie d'Adam et d'Eve* (1974) is a mine of information and detailed analysis. It gives a history of the text as well as a diplomatic edition of the manuscripts with a concordance. This thesis (Faculté Catholique de Strasbourg, 1972) discusses not only the Greek, but also the Latin, Georgian and Slavonic texts within the framework of the textual history of the Greek. There is a note on the Coptic, but Nagel did not yet know the Armenian *Penitence of Adam*.

Volume III of Nagel's dissertation presents the text of over twenty available Greek manuscripts printed synoptically in horizontal lines. Although he expresses definite views on the value of various groups of manuscripts for the reconstruction of the oldest retraceable text, Nagel has not given a critical text in his dissertation. He was preparing one but did not live to publish it; at the insistence of Father A.-M. Denis O.P. he allowed a preliminary text to be used in the latter's *Concordance grecque des pseudépigraphes d'Ancien Testament* (1987). This is the text printed in the first column of the Anderson-Stone *Synopsis* (1994).

D.A. Bertrand in his *La vie grecque d'Adam et Eve* (1987) makes good critical use of the Greek material collected by Nagel. He agrees with Nagel's assessment of the value of the manuscripts, and gives in each instance the oldest available text, provided he is able to make sense of it. In view of the great complexity of the textual tradition he lists only (in his view) the most important variants, and gives an eclectic translatable text. Comparing Nagel's preliminary text with that of Bertrand we understandably find a relatively great number of discrepancies. We still have no critical Greek text; hence not only the older, but also the most recent translations of the Greek have to be used with caution.

Editions and Translations

The editions of the Greek texts are:

C. Tischendorf, *Apocalypses Apocryphae* (Leipzig, 1866; repr. Hildesheim: Olms, 1966), pp. 1-23.

A.-M. Ceriani, in 'Apocalypsis Moysi in medio mutila', in *Monumenta Sacra et Profana. V.2. Opuscula et fragmenta miscella magnam partem apocrypha*, (Milan, 1868), pp. 19-24.

M. Nagel, *La vie d'Adam et d'Eve (Apocalypse de Moïse)*, I–III (Lille: Service de réproduction, Université de Lille III, 1974).

—preliminary edition in A.-M. Denis, *Concordance grecque des pseudépigraphes d'Ancien Testament* (Louvain-la-Neuve: Institut Orientaliste, 1987), pp. 815-18.

D.A. Bertrand, *La vie grecque d'Adam et Eve* (Recherches intertestamentaires, 1; Paris: Maisonneuve, 1987).

Among the translations (often accompanied by introductions and notes) we mention the following:

L.S.A. Wells, in R.H. Charles (ed.), *The Apocrypha and Pseudepigrapha of the Old Testament* (Oxford: Clarendon Press, 1913), II, pp. 123-54.

M.D. Johnson, in J.H. Charlesworth (ed.), *The Old Testament Pseudepigrapha* (Garden City, NY: Doubleday, 1983–85), II, pp. 249-95.

D.A. Bertrand, *La vie grecque d'Adam et Eve* (Recherches intertestamentaires, 1; Paris: Maisonneuve, 1987).

—in A. Dupont-Sommer and M. Philonenko (eds.), *La Bible, Ecrits Intertestamentaires* (Paris: Gallimard, 1987), pp. 1765-96.

C. Fuchs, in E. Kautzsch (ed.), *Die Apokryphen und Pseudepigraphen des Alten Testaments* (Tübingen, 1900; repr. Darmstadt: Wissenschaftliche Buchgesellschaft, 1962), pp. 506-28.

P. Riessler, in P. Riessler (ed.), *Altjüdisches Schrifttum ausserhalb der Bibel* (Heidelberg, 1928; repr. Darmstadt: Wissenschaftliche Buchgesellschaft, 1966), pp. 138-55.

N. Fernández Marcos, in A. Díez Macho (ed.), *Apócrifos del Antiguo Testamento* (Madrid: Ediciones Cristiandad, 1983), II, pp. 317-52.

The Latin *Life of Adam and Eve*

The situation with regard to the Latin *Life of Adam and Eve* is very unsatisfactory. There are two editions; one is over a hundred years old, and was made in 1878 by W. Meyer on the basis of twelve manuscripts, mainly from Munich, taking into account a number of mediaeval versions dependent on it. The second was published by J.H. Mozley in 1929; he used another twelve manuscripts found in British libraries. The latest list of availa ble manuscripts mentioned by Stone is that by M.B. Halford in 'The Apocryphal Vita Adae et Evae' (1981). It gives 73 items, but it seems likely that there are even more. In an abbreviated form Halford's list can be found in Stone, *History*, pp. 25-30.

Meyer distinguished between four groups of manuscripts. He usually followed group I, consisting of the three oldest manuscripts (from the ninth, tenth and twelfth century respectively) and giving the shortest form of the text, but he took into account variants in the other groups.

Group II gives some additions: the first is a prophecy concerning future events in ch. 29 of the Latin version, following Adam's remark that he has seen 'other mysteries' apart from those related in his vision (25.1–29.2). At the end of the document we again find a longer text, concerned with the tablets of stone and clay (mentioned in ch. 50 and in 51.3), on which Seth is supposed to have recorded the story of Adam and Eve, and which were allegedly found by Solomon when he built the temple. Group II was very influential in the history of the transmission of the text; many mediaeval translations and reworkings of the Latin version presuppose the text in the form found in this group. The manuscripts edited by Mozley also belong to it; eight of his manuscripts have yet other additions at the end, dealing with the formation of Adam's body and the giving of his name.

Group IV has the longer text found in group II in ch. 29 and after 51 (plus an extra phrase, also found in Mozley's manuscripts, but not the additions concerning the formation of Adam's body and the giving of his name).

Group III has the longer text in ch. 29, but nothing extra at the end of the document. It has a number of additions in chs. 42, 43, 44 and 48 that together present the legend of the Holy Rood. The archangel Michael gives Seth a twig from Paradise; he loses but regains it and gives it to Adam, who is very glad to see it. He enjoins Seth to plant it near his head on his grave; later it becomes a large tree that eventually supplies the wood of the cross.

Given the great diversity between the various forms of the Latin version the reconstruction of the oldest attainable text is a very difficult task. It should probably be preceded by the reconstruction of at least the principal individual text-forms, which are important in their own right as witnesses of the interplay between exegesis of the Bible and European mediaeval thinking and writing about Adam and Eve.

The text in the second column of the Anderson-Stone *Synopsis* was supplied by W. Lechner-Schmidt. It usually follows Meyer's group I, but also gives variant readings from other texts, including the long text in ch. 29, and the two additions at the end of the document (called chs. 52–54 and 55–57 respectively, following a suggestion by Mozley). It indicates the additions in group III, but does not give their text.

Translations of the Latin version are often presented together with translations of the Greek; see those by Wells, Johnson, Fuchs, and Fernández Marcos mentioned above (p. 13). Wells's translation of the Latin (together with that of the Greek of chs. 15–30) was revised by M. Whittaker (1984). Riessler gives his translation of the Latin separate from that of the Greek on pp. 668-81. All these translations mainly follow Meyer's group I, but some give the longer text in ch. 29, and other traditions (in full or in abstract) in the notes. Because of the lack of a critical edition, one should also use the translations of the Latin with caution.

Editions and Translations

The editions of the Latin *Vita* are the following:

W. Meyer, 'Vita Adae et Evae', *Abhandlungen der philosophisch-philologischen Klasse der königlichen Bayerischen Akademie der Wissenschaften*, XIV.3 (Munich, 1878), pp. 185-250.

J.H. Mozley, 'The "Vita Adae"', *JTS* 30 (1929), pp. 121-47.

See further on the Latin manuscript tradition:

M.B. Halford, 'The Apocryphal Vita Adae et Evae: Some Comments on the Manuscript Tradition', *Neuphilologische Mitteilungen* 82 (1981), pp. 417-27.

Translations of the Latin only:

P. Riessler, *Altjüdisches Schrifttum ausserhalb der Bibel* (Heidelberg, 1928; repr. Darmstadt: Wissenschaftliche Buchgesellschaft, 1966), pp. 668-881.

M. Whittaker, 'The Life of Adam and Eve', in H.F.D. Sparks (ed.), *The Apocryphal Old Testament* (Oxford: Clarendon Press, 1984), pp. 141-67.

The Armenian *Penitence of Adam*

The text of this writing was published in 1981 by M.E. Stone on the basis of three seventeenth-century manuscripts—see his *The Penitence of*

Adam. This document should be distinguished from the Armenian *Book of Adam*, which closely follows the Greek version as we know it and may be used as an additional witness for that version (for details see Stone, *History*, pp. 12-13). The translation of the *Penitence of Adam* is printed in the third column of the Anderson–Stone *Synopsis*.

Editions and Translations
M.E. Stone, *The Penitence of Adam* (CSCO, 429-30; Louvain: Peeters, 1981).

The Georgian *Book of Adam*
The Armenian *Penitence of Adam* is closely related to the Georgian *Book of Adam* published in 1964 by C'. K'urc'idze and translated by J.-P. Mahé in 1981 in his 'Le livre d'Adam géorgien'. This Georgian version is known from five manuscripts; four (three from the seventeenth century and one from the fifteenth or sixteenth) belong to a first recension, one (from the seventeenth century) to a second. Mahé follows the first recension and gives the text of the second only where the first is defective. In a later study ('Notes philologiques', 1983) Mahé has compared his text with that of Stone, and suggested some corrections in the Armenian with the help of the Georgian, and in the Georgian with the help of the Armenian. The Anderson-Stone Synopsis prints Mahé's translation of 1981 in its fourth column, with a number of corrections supplied by Mahé.

Editions and Translations
C'. K'urc'idze, 'Adamis apokrip'uli c'xovrebis k'art'uli versia', *P'ilologiuri dziebani* 1 (1964), pp. 97-136.

J.-P. Mahé, 'Le livre d'Adam géorgien' in R. van den Broek and M. J. Vermaseren (eds.), *Studies in Gnosticism and Hellenistic religions* (Festschrift G. Quispel; EPROER 91; Leiden: Brill, 1981), pp. 227-260.

—'Notes philologiques sur la version géorgienne de la Vita Adae', *Bedi Kartlisa, Revue de Kartvélologie* 41 (1983), pp. 51-66.

The Slavonic *Life of Adam and Eve*
For the Slavonic we are still dependent on the edition by V. Jagić in his 'Slavische Beiträge zu den biblischen Apocryphen' (1893). His translation of the longer of two existing recensions can be found in the last column of the Anderson-Stone *Synopsis*. Much new material, however, has come to light, duly listed in E. Turdeanu, 'La *Vie d'Adam et d'Eve* en slave et en roumain'. It is summarized and commented upon in Stone, *History*, pp. 30-36. Turdeanu thinks that the prototype of the longer recension was translated from the Greek in Western Macedonia

in the beginning of the fourteenth century. He also gives much information about the abbreviated second recension extant in three families and in two Romanian translations.

Editions and Translations

V. Jagić, 'Slavische Beiträge zu den biblischen Apocryphen, I, Die altkirchenslavischen Texte des Adambuches', *Denkschriften der kaiserlichen Akademie der Wissenschaften, Phil. Hist. Classe* 42.1 (Vienna, 1893), pp. 1-104.

E. Turdeanu, 'La *Vie d'Adam et d'Eve* en slave et en roumain', in his *Apocryphes slaves et roumains de l'Ancien Testament* (SVTP 5; Leiden: Brill, 1981), pp. 75-144 and 437-38.

Coptic fragments

Some fragments of Coptic versions are known. One, in Sahidic, published by W.E. Crum, fragmentarily covers the equivalent of Gr. 31–32 (W.E. Crum, *Catalogue of Coptic Manuscripts* [1909], n. 84); the other, in the Fayyumic dialect, offers fragments that largely agree with Gr. 28–29 (ed. J. Leipoldt, *Ägyptische Urkunden aus den königlichen Museen zu Berlin* [1904], n. 181). O.H.E. Burmester, in his catalogue of Coptic manuscripts in the University of Hamburg (1975), mentions two leaves of an Arabic text about the life of Adam from a Coptic monastery. However, the text was not published as announced, probably because of the author's demise, so that we are at present unable to comment on it. J. van der Vliet informs us that the Hamburg University Library now reports that the leaves are missing.

Stone mentions two additional Coptic texts which might reflect a Coptic version of the *Life of Adam and Eve*. Although one of these is somewhat closer to the *Life* than the other, they should both be ranged among the secondary Adam literature (see *The Discourse on Abbatôn*, in E.A.W. Budge, *Coptic Martyrdoms* [1914]; and *The Mysteries of the Apostle John and of the Holy Virgin*, in O.H.E. Burmester, 'Egyptian Mythology in the Coptic Apocrypha' [1938]).

Editions and Translations

E.A.W. Budge, 'The Discourse on Abbatôn', in: his *Coptic Martyrdoms etc. in the Dialect of Upper Egypt* (London: British Museum, 1914), pp. x-xi; xxii-xxiii; lxviii-lxxii (introductions and summary), pp. 225-49 (text) and pp. 482-91 (translation).

O.H.E. Burmester, 'Egyptian Mythology in the Coptic Apocrypha', *Orientalia* 7 (1938), pp. 355-67.

—*Koptische Handschriften 1: Die Handschriftenfragmente der Staats- und Universitätsbibliothek Hamburg* (VOHD, 21.1; Wiesbaden: Steiner, 1975), Suppl. 26, p. 305.

W.E. Crum, *Catalogue of Coptic Manuscripts in the Collection of the John Rylands Library* (Manchester: Manchester University Press, 1909), p. 40 n. 84.

J. Leipoldt, *Ägyptische Urkunden aus den königlichen Museen zu Berlin*, I (Berlin: Weidmann, 1904), pp. 171-72 n. 181.

The Contents of the Different Versions

Before discussing the problems of the relationships between the different versions (Chapter 2) and analysing their constitutive elements and main themes (Chapter 3), it will be useful to sketch the contents of these documents in broad outline. We shall first look at the individual versions (excepting, for obvious reasons, the scraps of the Coptic versions) and then give a table presenting their contents together in parallel columns. The Anderson-Stone *Synopsis* divides all the material extant in the different versions into 39 'pericopes'; we favour, however, a somewhat different and more refined division, both for the purpose of the survey in the present section and for the more detailed investigations later on.

Traditionally, the chapter and verse numbers in the Greek and the Latin differ. In their *Synopsis* Anderson and Stone follow the numbering of Wells's translation (see p. 13 above; for the Greek it has been modified slightly by Nagel). Where Armenian and Georgian run parallel to the Greek or the Latin, the Greek or Latin numbers are used; in cases where they run parallel to both, there are two sets of numbers. This seems, indeed, the best solution. Jagić introduced a separate division into chapters for the Slavonic; it is maintained in the *Synopsis*, but has little to commend it.

The Greek *Life of Adam and Eve*

The Greek version of *LAE* begins with an introduction, in which the main characters and the situation in which the story proper is set, are presented. This introduction relates that, after Adam and Eve left Paradise, Eve gave birth to two sons, Cain and Abel. After Cain has murdered Abel (as foreseen by Eve in a dream), Seth is born to replace Abel. Thus, the three main characters of the story, Adam, Eve and Seth, are introduced (chs. 1–4). Next, in the manner of a formal farewell speech, Adam's life is summarized by mentioning the number of his offspring (thirty sons and thirty daughters) and his age (930 years), and the farewell scene is evoked by the statements that he fell ill and gathered his children around him (chs. 5–6).

In order to explain the reason for his illness he tells the story of the Fall (chs. 7–8)—very briefly because Eve's account is still to follow in chs. 15–30. In chs. 9–13 Eve and Seth set out to try and get oil from Paradise to alleviate Adam's pains; interwoven is a story about an attack by an animal on Seth (chs. 10–12). Notwithstanding their urgent appeal Michael, sent by God, refuses to give Seth 'the oil of mercy'. He will not get any of it (13.1-3a) but has to return to his father who will die in three days. Seth will see Adam's soul leave his body and ascend to heaven (13.6; compare the story of Adam's death in chs. 31–42). After the failure of their mission Eve and Seth return to Adam, who blames Eve for bringing death upon humanity and asks her to tell the story of the Fall in more detail (ch. 14).

(Later somebody found the archangel's reply to Seth unsatisfactory; in a number of manuscripts [designated as ALCR, see below] we find a passage announcing the resurrection of 'all flesh' at the end of times [13.3b-5; compare 28.4].)

In chapters 15–30 we hear Eve's detailed story about the Fall, which has the form of a farewell discourse (see 15.1 and 30.1). After a description of the situation in Paradise (ch. 15), we hear how Satan seduced the serpent (ch. 16), and Eve through the serpent (chs. 17–19). Eve calls her husband, and through her mouth the devil speaks the words that seduce Adam (ch. 21). God descends to Paradise and summons Adam to render account for what he has done (chs. 22–23). Next, Adam, Eve, and the serpent are condemned for their actions (chs. 24–26). When the angels start expelling Adam and Eve from Paradise, Adam asks for mercy (ch. 27). His request to be allowed to eat from the tree of life is refused (ch. 28; there is, however, a reference to Adam's future resurrection in v. 4). A request to be allowed to take fragrances from Paradise so that they may bring offerings to God and God may hear them, is granted. Adam receives four kinds of fragrant spices and herbs, plus 'seeds for his food' (ch. 29). In chapter 30 Eve ends her story by admonishing her children: 'Watch yourselves so that you do not forsake the good.'

(Two manuscripts [designated as R and M; related to these manuscripts is the Slavonic version, see below] omit the references to 'the seeds for food' and add, instead, the story of Adam's and Eve's search for food after their expulsion from Paradise, and their decision to do penance, Adam by standing in the water of the river Jordan, and Eve by standing in the Tigris. Adam fulfills this purpose but Eve is deceived by the devil for a second time [29.7-13]. All this is found, in a more elaborate form, at the beginning of the Armenian *Penitence of Adam*, the Georgian *Book of Adam* and the Latin *Life of Adam and Eve* [see below].)

The *Greek Life of Adam and Eve* ends with an elaborate account of the death of Adam and Eve. Eve bewails the dying Adam and confesses her sins. An angel announces that she will witness the assumption of Adam's spirit (chs. 31–32). Indeed, she watches a chariot of light descending to the place where Adam is lying and angels sacrificing frankincense and praying on Adam's behalf (ch. 33). Eve asks Seth to join her and together they watch the events that follow: amongst others they see two figures, who prove to be the sun and the moon, whose light has faded in the presence of God, the father of all light (chs. 34–36). God forgives Adam, the angels praise him for it, a seraph washes Adam in the Acherusian Lake and God commands Michael to bring Adam to Paradise in the third heaven until the final judgment (ch. 37).

Another story, this time concerned with the burial of Adam's body, follows. God descends on earth on his chariot (ch. 38; Seth is the only human witness of this and the following events) and speaks with Adam, promising him that in the eschatological future he will make Adam sit on the throne which the devil used to occupy (ch. 39). Angels prepare Adam's body for his funeral in the region of Paradise (on earth); an excursus explains why Abel is buried only now, together with his father (ch. 40). God again speaks to Adam's body promising his own resurrection and that of all his descendants (ch. 41). God seals Adam's tomb and all celestials return to heaven (42.1-2). Eve dies and Seth buries her, instructed by Michael, in Adam's grave (42.1–43.1). Before ascending to heaven Michael adds instruction about the burial of all human beings (43.2-5).

The structure of the *Greek Life of Adam and Eve* can schematically be presented as follows.

   1–4 Introduction: Presentation of the main characters, Adam, Eve and Seth
   5–8 Setting of the farewell scene; Adam's account of the fall
   9–14 Eve's and Seth's futile quest for medicine for Adam
   15–30 Eve's account of the fall
   31–37 Adam's death and assumption
   38–43 Adam's burial, and Eve's death and burial

The Armenian and Georgian Versions

The Armenian and the Georgian texts show a number of differences, but they clearly go back to a common *Vorlage* (see Chapter 2, p. 35 below). They can, therefore, be discussed together in this section.

In these two versions Adam and Eve, expelled from Paradise, become hungry after seven days and start looking for food (chs. 1–2; because of the parallel with the Latin [see below] the Latin numbering is followed here). They find nothing similar to the food they used to eat in Paradise, and they decide to do penance so that God may give them better food than that fit for animals (chs. 3–4). Adam will do penance for forty days, Eve for thirty-four—she standing up to her neck in the Tigris, he in the Jordan (chs. 5–7). All goes well with Adam, but Eve is seduced by the devil who tells her that God has given heed to their penitence and has granted forgiveness (chs. 8–9). He brings her to Adam who, of course, understands what has happened, accuses Satan and asks him why he is so hostile towards them (chs. 10–11).

Satan then tells the story of his own fall. He refused to worship Adam, created in the likeness of God's image, and even made the other angels follow his example. God expelled him and the others from their heavenly dwelling and cast them down to the earth (chs. 12–16).

Adam asks God to remove his adversary and the devil becomes invisible (17.1-2). Eve, acknowledging her responsibility for the first and the second sin, goes to the west, pregnant with Cain (17.3–18.3). Her cry for help at her parturition miraculously reaches Adam, who is allowed to leave the water and to go to Eve in order to help her (chs. 19–20). (We are told that God heeds Adam's penitence, and Michael brings him seeds and teaches him sowing and reaping [20.1].) Adam prays for Eve and an angel acts as midwife while Cain is born (ch. 21).

From this point onwards the type of text jointly represented by Arm. and Georg. by and large agrees with the Greek version (and we shall from here on use the chapter division of the Greek). There are some minor differences, generally offering a clearer and more consistent story-line than the Greek (for some details, see ch. 2 below). Also, Arm. and Georg. have an explicitly Christian character.

Adam's concise story of the fall (chs. 7–8) is fuller than that of the Greek; apocryphal details, present in Eve's account of the Fall, are in Arm. and Georg. given here already; but also in Eve's account, for example in chs. 16 and 17, the text is more detailed and clearer. On the other hand, the 'seeds for food', given to Adam according to the Greek ch. 29, are not mentioned in Arm. and Georg., for these versions have related the search for food already in full in their chs. 1–21.

In the Armenian version, the story of Adam's assumption (33.1–38.1) is absent. It is present, however, in the Georgian version, so that we must assume that the common ancestor of Arm. and Georg. had a text parallel to the one in the Greek version. The absence in Arm. may be accidental (due to a leap from one descending chariot in ch. 33 to the other in ch. 38) or deliberate. In any case, the common ancestor of Arm. and Georg. does not diverge importantly from the Greek in this last section of the document.

Explicit Christian elements are found in the prophecy concerning the future resurrection, located in 13.3b-5, where the Greek manuscripts ALCR have a related, but different prophecy; in God's condemnation of the serpent (ch. 26), there is a reference to the cross of God's son; and in the prediction of the final day (ch. 37), Georg. mentions God's 'beloved Son'.

The structure of the Armenian and Georgian versions of the Life of Adam and Eve can schematically be presented as follows.

> (Lat. 1–2) Introduction:
>   Adam's and Eve's lack of food outside Paradise
> (Lat. 3–11) The penitence of Adam and Eve, and Eve's second seduction
> (Lat. 12–17) The story of the devil's fall
> (Lat. 17–21) The birth of Cain
> Gr. 1–4 (Lat. 22–24) Cain kills Abel; Seth is born
> Gr. 5–8 (Lat. 30–34) Farewell scene; Adam's illness; his account of the fall
> Gr. 9–14 (Lat. 35–44) Eve's and Seth's futile quest for medicine for Adam
> Gr. 15–30 (absent in Lat.) Eve's account of the fall
> Gr. 31–37 (Lat. 45–47) Adam's death (and assumption, in Georg. only)
> Gr. 38–43 (Lat. 48–51) Adam's burial, and Eve's death and burial

The Latin *Life of Adam and Eve*

The Latin version begins in the same way as the Armenian and the Georgian. It shares with those versions the stories of Adam and Eve searching for food and their penitence in the Jordan and the Tigris, the account of the jealousy and the fall of Satan, and the story of the separation of Adam and Eve and the birth of Cain. A few times the Latin gives a longer text, but on the whole it is more concise.

The passage about the seeds given to Adam for food is at the end of these chapters, after Adam has taken Eve and Cain to the east (ch. 22). In this way, these chapters end where they began: with the need for food outside Paradise. As we have seen, the corresponding statement in Arm. and Georg. follows immediately after it has been told that God heeded Adam's penitence (ch. 20). In that version, it concluded the story of Adam's penitence only; the Latin version can therefore be seen as literarily more advanced. Lat. concurs with Arm. and Georg. in siding with the Greek chs. 1–4 from here on, but giving a fuller and clearer version of the events related.

After 24.2 (Gr. 5.1) the Latin version stands alone in having Adam relate to Seth a vision which he had after being expelled from Paradise. It consists of a meeting and conversation between Adam and God, and is reminiscent of elements in Gr. chs. 22–29 (with no equivalent in Latin). The vision emphasizes that Adam's descendants will forever have the right and the duty to serve God, who has to be praised because of his great mercy (chs. 25–28). Adam asks Seth to listen also to 'other future mysteries and sacraments revealed to me, which by eating of the tree of knowledge I knew and understood, which shall be in this age' (29.2). What follows is not found in Meyer's group I, but the original text cannot have ended here.

(In the other groups of manuscripts the predictions take the form of a historical apocalypse describing various episodes in the history of Israel according to a 'Sin–Exile–Return' pattern. At the end there will be a period in which God will dwell among men on earth and all men will perform his commandments. Sins will be purified by water, we are told [29.9-10]; in its present form this apocalypse is Christian.)

In chs. 30–44 (Gr. 5–14) the Latin runs again parallel to the Greek, like Arm. and Georg. In the main it stands nearer to Arm.–Georg. than to Greek, but often it gives a somewhat smoother text than these two (for instance in chs. 32–34 [Gr. 7–8]). Interestingly the beast that attacks Seth in chs. 35–39 (Gr. 10–12) is identified as a serpent, and addressed as 'accursed enemy of truth'. In chs. 41–43 (Gr. 13.3-5) Latin has its own, equally Christian, version of the prophecy found in Arm.–Georg. at this point. It is identical with a passage in the Latin translation of the *Gospel of Nicodemus* (ch. 19 = *Descensus ad Inferos* 3). Eve and Seth return to Adam 'carrying with them sweet-smelling herbs—nard, crocus, calamus and cinnamon' (43.2, compare Gr. 19.6).

(At this point, as well as earlier in ch. 42 and later in ch. 44, the manuscripts belonging to group III have a number of additions concerned with episodes of the Legend of the Holy Rood.)

In ch. 44 (Gr. 14) the story as told by the Latin version takes a different turn. Adam asks Eve to tell to her children the story of the Fall and its consequences, *but after his death*. Consequently Eve's 'farewell discourse' (Gr. chs. 15–30) is not found in Latin; after a short version of the account of Adam's death and burial, we find, however, a farewell speech of Eve in chs. 49–50, that is not found in any of the other versions. As for the account of Adam's death, there is a short farewell-speech of Adam to his children (ch. 45). Sun, moon and stars darken for seven days, the whole family mourns, and Seth is invited to watch what God has in store for his creature, on whom he has pity (ch. 46). We read how the angels praise God for his mercy (ch. 47) and then the story of the burial of Adam and Abel follows (ch. 48, compare Gr. ch. 40). (Here the manuscri pts of group III add the concluding episodes of the Legend of the Holy Rood.)

In Lat. 49–50 Eve tells about Michael's announcement to Adam and herself of a judgment first with water and then by fire. She commands her children to make tablets of stone and of clay with the story of the life of Adam and Eve which they have just heard and seen—so that the story can survive one way or another. Eve dies and is buried by her children. After four days of mourning Michael appears to Seth (ch. 51, comp. Gr. ch. 43) with the message not to mourn more than six days, 'because on the seventh day is the sign of the resurrection and the rest of the age to come'. In the shortest version of the Latin text (found in groups I and III) the document ends with the words: 'Then Seth made the tablets.' In the manuscripts of Meyer's group II and IV a long addition follows, and other manuscripts add even more (see p. 14 above).

The structure of the shortest Latin version of the *Life of Adam and Eve* can schematically be presented as follows.

1–2 Introduction: Adam's and Eve's lack of food outside Paradis
3–11 The penitence of Adam and Eve, and Eve's second seduction
12–17 The story of the devil's fall
17–21 The birth of Cain
22–24 Cain kills Abel; Seth is born
25–29 Adam relates his vision to Seth
30–34 Adam's illness; his account of the fall
35–44 Eve's and Seth's futile quest for medicine for Adam
45–48 Adam's death, assumption and burial
49–51 Eve's farewell speech, death, and burial

The Slavonic Version

The Slavonic version begins with a short statement concerning Adam's authority over the animals in Paradise before the Fall. In none of the other versions do we find a parallel to this. It then proceeds with describing what happened after Adam's and Eve's expulsion from Paradise, in a free version of Gr. chs. 1–4. Next follows the equivalent of Gr. chs. 5–14, with the Slavonic keeping rather close to the Greek. In the parallel to Gr. ch. 7 it emphasizes that Eve was deceived because the devil changed himself into an angel, and that the serpent acted in a very clever manner. It should be noted that Slav., in agreement with the main Greek tradition, offers a short text in Gr. ch. 13 and does not contain the prophecies found in the Greek manuscripts ALCR or any of the other versions (see above, pp. 19, 22 and 23). It does mention, however, that Seth receives three twigs (of the fir, the cedar and the cypress), of which Adam makes a crown for his head (compare the addition of elements from the Holy Rood legend in the Latin group III at this point).

Of the farewell discourse of Eve in Gr. chs. 15–30 Slav. gives a special version. The stories of the temptation of the serpent, of Eve and of Adam are told very briefly (Gr. chs. 16–21). God then summons Adam and takes him to task. There is no equivalent of the words to Adam, Eve and the serpent individually in Gr. 24–26, and the story immediately moves to the expulsion from Paradise in Gr. 27. We should note here that the Greek manuscript R also jumps from 23.3 to 27.1, and that its companion manuscript M has a similar omission (see above, p. 19). Adam's prayer for mercy is followed by his request for food and sweet incenses (Gr. 29.3-6). He receives only the sweet incenses.

Like R and M, the Slavonic does not tell us anything about seeds for food given to Adam at this occasion. With the Greek manuscripts this version adds here the story of Adam and Eve's search for food and their penitence in the Jordan and the Tigris respectively. The chain of events, however, is different in the Slavonic, and a number of events, not known from R and M or from other versions, precedes the penitence of Adam and Eve. After Adam and Eve have prayed at the entrance of Paradise for fifteen days, God sends the archangel Joel, who gives one seventh of paradise to Adam and Eve, so that Adam will be able to till the ground covered with thistles and thorns, and then allows him to tame animals. This is followed by the story of a contract between Adam and the devil. When Adam starts plowing the earth with the help of oxen, the devil comes and asks his due, claiming to be the lord of the earth. Adam cunningly assents to sign a contract with him in which he pledges allegiance to the Lord of the earth, acknowledging, however, God as the real Lord, and knowing, moreover, that this God will come on earth in human form and destroy the devil. In the meantime Adam and Eve decide to do penance. The story of that penance interestingly ends with a victory, also for Eve. The devil does not succeed in seducing Eve for a second time. She recognizes who is speaking to her and keeps silent. Adam rejoices greatly in her steadfastness and helps her to get out of the water.

In the chapters devoted to the account of the death of Adam and Eve (Gr. chs. 31–43) the Slavonic gives a much shorter text than the Greek. The text is even more concise than that found in the Greek manuscripts R and M. All that is found in Slav. is an announcement by Adam that he is to die, and a request to Eve to pray (compare Gr. 31), Eve's prayer (Gr. 32), offerings of incense at Adam's body and prayers in heaven, witnessed by Eve and Seth (Gr. 33.4–36.3), the washing of Adam's body in the Acherusian Lake and God's command to bury

Adam's body in Paradise and to let his spirit stay in the third heaven, until the resurrection (Gr. 37.1-6a). A short, smooth account of Adam's burial follows (Gr. 40–42; there is no excursus on Abel's burial here, although his grave is mentioned further on), and the story of Eve's death and burial is equally brief. This version is concluded by Michael's instructions to Seth about mourning rituals and by Joel's glorification of the Lord.

The structure of the Slavonic version of the Life of Adam and Eve can schematically be presented as follows (the numbers between brackets refer to the Slavonic chapters).

(1) Introduction. Situation: Adam was happy in Paradise, but was expelled after his sins

Gr. 1–4 (2–4) Adam's vision of Cain killing Abel; the birth of these sons and the murder; birth of Seth

Gr. 5–8 (5–10) Adam's illness and his account of the fall

Gr. 9–14 (11–17) Eve's and Seth's futile quest for medicine for Adam

Gr. 15–29 (18–27) Eve's account of the fall

[Gr. 29.7-13] (28–39) Eve's speech continued: Adam's and Eve's hunger, God's mercy; their contract with the devil, and their penitence

Gr. 31–42 (40–47) Adam's death, assumption and burial

Gr. 42–43 (48–50) Eve's last words, her death and burial. Conclusion

Table

This table lists the contents of the different versions in parallel columns.

x   a parallel section

(x)   a more remote parallel

pt   only extant in part of the manuscripts of the particular version

For details see the text of this chapter.

Content of section	Gr.	Arm.	Georg.	Lat.	Slav.
Situation: after the expulsion from Paradise	x	x	x	x	
Adam's authority over the animals					x
Adam and Eve searching for proper food		x	x	x	
Penitence in Jordan and Tigris; second temptation		x	x	x	
Story of jealousy and fall of devil		x	x	x	
Separation of Adam and Eve; birth of Cain		x	x	x	
Birth of (Cain and) Abel; death of Abel; birth of Seth	x	x	x	x	x
Vision of Adam (related to Seth)				x	
Prophecy concerning future events (idem)				pt	

Adam's illness; children assemble	x	x	x	x	x
Adam's account of the fall	x	x	x	x	x
Eve's and Seth's quest for oil from Paradise;					
Encounter with the Beast	x	x	x	x	x
Michael refuses request	x	x	x	x	x
Prediction of future resurrection	pt	x	x	x	
The Holy Rood				pt	
Return to Adam; rebuke of Eve	x	x	x	x	x
Portions of Adam and Eve in Paradise	x	x	x		x
Temptation of the serpent	x	x	x		x
Temptation of Eve	x	x	x		x
Temptation of Adam	x	x	x		x
Setting of the stage for judgment	x	x	x		x
Condemnation of Adam	x	x	x		
Condemnation of Eve	x	x	x		
Condemnation of serpent	x	x	x		
Expulsion. Adam asks for mercy	x	x	x		x
Second request of Adam: to eat from the tree					
of life (promised for time of resurrection)	x	x	x		
Third request of Adam: sweet incense for					
prayer to God (he receives four kinds)	x	x	x		x
(plus seeds for food)	x				
Adam and Eve searching for food	pt				x
Joel gives land to till and animals to tame					x
Contract with devil					x
Penitence in Jordan and Tigris;	pt				x
Second temptation	pt				x
Adam's death	x	x	x	x	x
Eve's prayer of confession	x	x	x		x
Vision of Eve and Seth; angelic liturgy	x		x	x	x
Assumption of Adam into Paradise	x		x		(x)
Short introduction to burial of Adam				x	
Story of burial of Adam and Abel					
near Paradise	x	x	x	x	(x)
The Holy Rood legend				pt	
Last words of Eve; command concerning					
tablets				x	
Eve's prayer before death	x	x	x		x
Eve's funeral. Epilogue	x	x	x	x	x
History of the tablets				pt	
Formation of Adam's body				pt	
Place of Adam's creation; his name				pt	

2

THE RELATIONSHIP BETWEEN
THE VARIOUS VERSIONS AND TEXT-FORMS

The Problems and the Ways to Solve Them

The surveys in the second part of the preceding chapter have shown that the five versions of the *Life of Adam and Eve* analysed there have much in common but show considerable differences at the same time. Next, that there are also divergencies between the various forms of text within the particular versions. This is, for instance, the case in the Greek—see the addition of Adam's and Eve's penitence in manuscripts R and M in 29.7-13—and in the Latin with the additions in groups II, III, IV, separately and jointly. In the case of the Slavonic, scholars usually go no further back than the recension reconstructed and translated by Jagić, but Turdeanu's survey of the available material (see Chapter 1, pp. 16-17) suggests a considerable inner-Slavonic variety.

The relationships between all these recensions and versions may be described in various ways. Stone (*History*, pp. 61-71) has made notable remarks on the methodological intricacies in any attempt to trace the development of such writings as the *Life of Adam and Eve*, and he has also presented some solutions offered in the history of research.

In this chapter we shall attempt to describe the development of the primary Adam literature, on the basis of which we believe the emergence of all extant recensions can be explained. Our theory takes into account that ancient literature such as the *Life of Adam and Eve* has been subject, in the centuries of its transmission, to constant adaptation by 'authors' or 'redactors', each with their own views and interests, resulting in more or less independent writings, worthy, at least, of independent study.

In a sense, this description of *LAE*'s development is premature, anticipating much research still to be done. The following *desiderata* may be mentioned.

(1) A fresh examination of the textual evidence available for the different versions is urgently needed. Thanks to Nagel we are in a relatively good position with regard to the Greek, but it is much to be regretted that he was not in a position to crown his labours with the reconstruction of a critical text. The editions of the Armenian and Georgian are based on relatively few manuscripts, and hence the situation is less complicated than in the case of the other versions. Yet if they would be studied afresh, with an eye to their reciprocal connections and the relationships with the Greek and the Latin, progress could be made. A new edition of the Latin, sifting the great mass of available material and arranging it in text-forms, is urgently needed. The same applies, perhaps to a lesser extent, also to the Slavonic.

(2) This crucial text-critical work, eventually leading to the reconstruction of the history of the text of the individual versions, should go hand in hand with the literary critical study of the relationships between the various text-forms within a given part of the tradition. The latter line of investigation is inseparable from text criticism because of the numerous additions and omissions in individual manuscripts. Moreover, as Stone has remarked (*History*, pp. 42-43), it is generally accepted that the versions known to us eventually derive from some Greek text-form. This poses the question of the relationships between the Greek *Vorlagen* of the Latin, Armenian and Georgian versions, and the Greek *Life* as we know it. Thus literary criticism is needed again, in this case as a study of the relationships between the forms of text represented by the versions themselves. Eventually this will lead to a survey of the developments within the entire textual tradition, and to an effort to reconstruct the oldest form of text.

(3) Particularly the common elements between the various forms in which the *Life of Adam and Eve* has been transmitted, lead us to survey the developments with a view to finding the form of text at the beginning of the whole complicated process of tradition. This is the subject of the second section of this chapter. But there is more to be done. Those who transmitted the different forms of the *Life of Adam and Eve* felt they could deal somewhat freely with the text before them. Not only did they feel free to vary in details of vocabulary and syntax, but they also omitted clauses or even entire pericopes, or inserted elements known to them from elsewhere. Thus a close analysis of the documents themselves, as writings presenting their story with a special *Tendenz* to

a particular audience, is needed. We have to pay special attention to the elements constitutive for the particular writings and their main themes (hence Chapter 3 below).

(4) Finally, there is scope for tradition criticism. We shall have to trace the history of traditions found in all (or practically all) versions of the *Life of Adam and Eve*, and also of those found in the individual text forms (or even those in individual manuscripts). Individual traditions and clusters of them should thus be compared to those found elsewhere, not only in the secondary Adam literature, but also in other Jewish and Christian sources that tried to interpret various aspects of the first chapters of Genesis, e.g. Jewish haggadic, exegetical and mystical literature and Christian exegetical and homiletical writings. In doing this one will have to keep in mind that, to some extent, the study of the development of the traditions incorporated in the different versions is independent of the study of the history of the writings themselves.

In all this we should realize that we are dealing with a mediaeval manuscript tradition, and the themes and traditions found in our literature require the attention of mediaevalists specializing in different geographical areas and in different aspects of Western and Eastern civilization (including mediaeval art), as well as of scholars who are acquainted with Jewish traditions between, say, 200 before to 400 after the beginning of the Common Era, and of specialists concerned with early Christianity.

The Relationships between the Textual Witnesses

In this section it will be argued that the Greek version represented by manuscripts DSV (K)PG B was the fountainhead of all subsequent development of the writing in its various recensions. The present authors like to think of themselves as unprejudiced students, untainted by the superstition of the *graeca veritas*, which is intuitively inclined to regard what is preserved in Greek as 'more original' than what is preserved in, for instance, a Georgian translation. This intuition is fundamentally misleading. Nonetheless, the reconstruction offered below is capable of describing the extant versions of the *Life of Adam and Eve* as the results of an organic process that was primarily driven by the need to clarify, and the wish to amplify, previous stages of the writing. The extant Greek *Life of Adam and Eve* represents, in our opinion, the oldest retraceable stage of this process, accounting for all other versions.

The following stages will be considered:

1. The relationships between the Greek manuscripts.
2. The Armenian and Georgian versions in relation to the Greek.
3. The Latin version compared to the Armenian and the Georgian, and to the Greek.
4. The Greek manuscripts R and M and the Slavonic version.
5. The Coptic fragments.
6. The earliest stages of a complex tradition process.

The Relationships between the Greek Manuscripts

In his dissertation Nagel lists 29 manuscripts, 23 of which he could use. Bertrand mentions the same manuscripts, but uses only 21 for a selective apparatus on his eclectic text. In the meantime there seems to be one additional witness: A.-M. Denis has drawn our attention to the fact that F. Schmidt (*Le Testament d'Abraham*, p. 25) records that in manuscript Sinai Gr. 431 (of the fifteenth century) *GLAE* precedes the *Testament of Abraham* (beginning on fol. 80v.).

Nagel describes all manuscripts in great detail, but his study is not always easy to consult. Bertrand (*La vie grecque*, pp. 40-47) gives a handy survey of the essential information. He has introduced somewhat simpler sigla for the manuscripts than those used by Nagel, and Stone has rightly suggested that one should use these from now onward. On p. 10 of his *History* we find a convenient synoptic table of the sigla used by Tischendorf, J.L. Sharpe (in an unpublished PhD dissertation [Duke University, 1969] used by M.D. Johnson in *The Old Testament Pseudepigrapha*), Nagel and Bertrand.

On the whole the transmission of the text is very free; there are numerous changes in diction and many additions and omissions, both redactional and accidental. Determining the oldest recoverable text in detail is a very difficult task. Nagel distinguishes between three major text forms in the Greek: form I is subdivided in four groups: DSV, KPG, B, and ATLC; form II consists of manuscript R and M; form III is subdivided in three groups: NI(J)K (J being a copy of I), QZ, and HEWXF. Bertrand follows Nagel in this classification. We shall briefly characterize these text-forms.

The *first* text-form is represented by eleven manuscripts, in four groups. Nagel lists them as DSV K(belongs here for 14.3–43.5)PG B ATLC. In his opinion DSV represent the least corrupted text. D, an eleventh-century palimpsest, is the oldest extant witness (= manuscript Milan, Bibl. Ambr. C 237 inf., fol. 78v-84r). Unfortunately it has a large lacuna, omitting chs. 18–35, and several portions of text have become badly readable or not readable at all. Fortunately some may be recovered from the edition of this manuscript by A.-M. Ceriani in 'Apocalypsis Moysi in medio mutila'. The text in S (= manuscript Strasbourg, BNU 1913, fol. 68r-76v, dating from the thirteenth to the fourteenth century) is closely related to that in D, and gives us valuable supplementary information. Finally V (= manuscript Athos, Vatopedi 422, fol. 13v-20v, from the thirteenth century) can be used as an additional witness in the reconstruction of the common ancestor of DS on the one hand and V on the other.

KPG are fragmentary and, it seems, of little importance. Manuscript B is a free paraphrase of the first text-form.

The ATLC group gives the first form of text with some important additions. Its oldest representatives, A and C, date from the thirteenth to the fourteenth and from the thirteenth century respectively (compare S and V). Nagel rightly observes the 'key-position' of ATLC in the transmission of the writing (*La vie grecque* I, p. 47).

The text found in ATLC is secondary to that of the other representatives of the first form. Nagel regards a process of addition in the different forms of text (found in the Greek manuscripts as well as in the other versions) more likely than one of omission. In connection with ATLC he remarks that it is inconceivable that these manuscripts would have preserved primitive readings that other witnesses of the same form of text would have lost (on this matter, see Nagel, *La vie grecque* I, pp. 47-51).

The *second* form of the text (represented by the Greek manuscripts R and M) derives from the ATLC group, and in its turn this text-form engendered the Slavonic version. But also the Latin version, and the common ancestor of the Armenian and Georgian versions presuppose the longer ATLC text.

The theory of the secondary nature of the passages with a longer text in ATLC is corroborated by the fact that its additions are not found in the *third* form of text, represented by the manuscripts NI(J)K(for title-17.2) QZ HEWXF. In this group of manuscripts (or in one of its subgroups) we find a number of secondary additions and other alterations not found elsewhere. In this group the Armenian *Book of Adam* (see Chapter 1, p. 16) finds a place; it is especially connected with NI(J)K.

Bertrand, following Nagel's order of preference in his edition of the text, usually gives the text represented by DSV and others, and not that of ATLC, at least as far as, in his opinion, the former makes good sense. Contrary to what one would expect, Nagel, in his text for A.-M. Denis's *Concordance*, follows the ATLC text in many cases. Probably he just wanted to include all material that he regarded as ancient; he also gives the text of 29.7-13, reconstructed from R and M.

Some representative examples may serve to illustrate the differences between the various families of the Greek textual traditions, and why the alterations were made. To begin with, we mention a few of the additions in ATLC, plus (in some cases) R and M, which betray the tendency to amplify or clarify the shorter text.

In 5.3 Adam's sons gather after he has fallen ill and has summoned them. At the end of the verse A(T)L(C)R add: 'they came to the door of the house where he entered to pray to God' (a reading also found in Georg. and very probably presupposed in Arm. and Lat.). This addition was probably made only because the author of the ATLC text knew the tradition that Adam had this private prayer-house (this tradition is also present in, for example, the *Cave of Treasures* 5.17 and may be very old; see below, Chapter 5, p. 86).

In 8.1 ATLCR add that God, when he entered Paradise after Adam's fall, 'placed his throne'. This addition is explicable from the wish to give a fuller text. The mention of the throne is possibly intended to evoke the environment of a court-room, for immediately after this remark, God starts interrogating Adam.

In 9.3 Adam sends out Eve and Seth to ask for the oil from Paradise so that he may get relief from his pains. He says, 'then I shall anoint myself and shall have rest from my complaints'. AT(L)CR(M) add: 'and I shall show you the manner in which we were deceived formerly' (so also Arm. and Georg.). This phrase is meant to explain why Adam, failing to get what he needs, asks Eve to tell the story of their transgression in his stead (14.3). In fact, he sleeps while she tells it and dies a day later (31.1).

In 12.2 the beast, after declaring to Seth that he will withdraw from the image of God, goes to his lair. In an attempt to bring this peculiar episode to a more satisfactory, in this case, less anti-climactic conclusion, ATL specify that the beast 'left Seth wounded (lit. struck, smitten)'.

A particular case is the longer text found in ACLR in 13.3-5 (already mentioned in Chapter 1, p. 19). Michael refuses the oil to Seth and tells him: 'It shall not be yours now, but you go back again to your father, for the measure of his life is fulfilled.' The 'now' made people wonder what would happen later. Hence the addition 'but at the end

of times' in ACLR, introducing a prophecy concerning the resurrection of 'all flesh from Adam to that great day', forming a holy people
sharing in the joy of Paradise. God will be in their midst, they will sin
no longer, but will receive a new heart in order to serve the one God.
This view on the future corresponds with God's promises to Adam in
ch. 28, towards the end of the 'Farewell discourse of Eve'.

With regard to NI(J)K QZ HEWF we may point to the framework
and the beginning of Eve's story in 14.3–16.3. In 14.2 Adam is said to
exclaim: 'O Eve, what have you done? You have brought a great
wrath upon us, namely death which rules over our entire race.'
According to the main Greek tradition he continues in 14.3 by com-
manding his wife to explain to their children how all this came about.
She does this, while Adam sleeps (31.1).

In this text-form the framework of Eve's speech is thoroughly
reworked. In this version, Eve reacts to Adam's accusation by blaming
the serpent (compare Gen. 3.13); then she and Adam weep together,
and finally Adam falls asleep. Their children spontaneously gather
around his bed and, while they are weeping over Adam, Eve decides to
relate to them what exactly happened. The story she tells agrees largely
with her speech according to the other manuscripts. Only in the first
lines of Eve's story the situation is somewhat simplified. The references
to the Eastern and Western parts of Paradise, for instance, are left out
(and the text in 17.3, about the 'guarding' of these parts is adapted
accordingly), and the reason why the devil wanted to have Adam and
Eve thrown out of Paradise is clarified. From 16.3b this text-form
rejoins the main tradition. The closing part of this scene, however, is
also changed. When Eve has finished speaking, she weeps again with
her children. After that, Adam wakes up (31.1) and the following
scenes agree again with those in the main tradition.

The changes just mentioned seem to have been made for aesthetic
reasons only (so also Nagel, *La vie grecque* I, p. 213). Although the third
text-form is somewhat less harsh on Eve, the overall tendency has not
changed.

From this survey, it can be concluded that the 'short' text-form, that
is, the text-form represented by DSV (K)PG B, contains the oldest
form of the *Life of Adam and Eve* known to us. It is most likely that the
extras *vis-à-vis* the first text-form in manuscripts ATLC, as well as in
the second and third text-forms, are secondary additions. In the following sections, we shall suggest that the Armenian, Georgian and Latin
text-forms eventually derive from the ATLC group, and that the

Slavonic is closely related to the form of the text in manuscripts R and M. The third form of the Greek text does not seem to have left its traces in the ensuing history of the text and its versions.

The Armenian and Georgian Versions in relation to the Greek

Research by M.E. Stone and J.-P. Mahé (summarized in Stone, *History*, pp. 36-39; 69) has established that the Armenian and the Georgian version are closely related. They go back to a common Greek ancestor related to the ATLC group of Greek manuscripts. However, as we have seen (in Chapter 1, pp. 20-21), they begin with the stories of (a) Adam and Eve looking for food; (b) the penitence of Adam and Eve; (c) the fall of the devil; (d) the separation of Adam and Eve, and Cain's birth— as the Latin *Life of Adam and Eve*. After this, they have an adapted version of the beginning chs. 1–4 in the Greek.

The Georgian is not directly dependent on the Armenian; it does not share, for instance, the long omission in the Armenian of the equivalent of Gr. 33.1–38.1. Nor is the Armenian dependent on the Georgian; it does not join it in leaving out the equivalent of Gr. 20.1-3. The differences between Arm. and Georg. can be explained in various ways. First, either of the persons who first translated the documents into Armenian or Georgian may have dealt freely with the text before them. It is also possible that the translators had different Greek *Vorlagen*, both dependent on one common ancestor, but in practice more different *Vorlagen* cannot be traced. Probably also at least some of the changes were introduced during the subsequent transmission of the texts in Armenian and Georgian.

A detailed comparison of these two versions by specialists is urgently needed. We have to list the readings peculiar to either of them (or to their particular *Vorlage*), and to determine which readings are distinctive for the type of text they jointly represent. This should then be followed by a comparison of the text of the common ancestor of Armenian and Georgian versions with the Greek (ATLC), and later also with the Latin.

In the meantime a few things may be said on the basis of the now available evidence. With due caution, given also the lack of specialist knowledge on the part of the present authors, some cases may be selected to illustrate the relationship between Arm., Georg. and Gr. On the whole, in our opinion, the differences between Arm.–Georg. and Gr. point to attempts of the former to clarify the story found in the Greek (see also Chapter 1, p. 21).

In 7.2 Adam, in his story of the Fall, tells his children, according to the Greek text: 'And the hour drew near for the angels who were guarding your mother to ascend and worship the Lord. And the enemy gave to her, and she ate from the tree, because he knew that neither I nor the holy angels were near her. Then she gave also me to eat.' The beginning of v. 2 obviously called for an explanation, and that is given in Arm. and Georg. In the passage just quoted they first give a somewhat shorter story, but they add that Adam ate not realizing what was given to him. Then they explain that Adam and Eve guarded different parts of the Garden, each helped by twelve angels, who every day went up to worship God (comp. 15.2 and 17.1 in the longer story of Eve in chs. 15–30). Arm. (followed by Georg.) continues: 'at that time Satan deceived your mother and caused her to eat of the fruit; Satan knew that I was not with her, nor the angels, at that time he caused her to eat. Afterwards she gave it to me (Georg. adds: and I did not understand).' Before and after the excursus on the function of the angels, we are told that Satan gave Eve to eat and that Eve gave the fruit to Adam. This is an indication that the explanation was added later. It is also found in the Latin version of this passage, but without the duplication just mentioned (see also p. 38 below).

In 13.3b-5 Arm. and Georg. expand and change the prophecy concerning the future resurrection found in ALCR. It is not easy to reconstruct the common text behind both versions, but it is clear that it goes back to an effort by Christians to supplement and Christianize the story. Instead of '(not now) but at the end of times' Arm. reads: 'but then, at the end of time when the years of the end are filled and completed, then the beloved Christ will come to resurrect Adam's body because of his sins which took place'. Georg. has a similar text, but adds that this will be 'à la cinq millième année et demi'. This corresponds with '5500 years' in the Latin version (and in both the Greek *Gospel of Nicodemus* and its Latin translation, see also Chapter 1, p. 23 as well as pp. 38-39 below). It should be noted that 5500 years feature regularly in computations of the end of time. In the *Cave of Treasures* 52, and in the *Discourse on Abbatôn*, the 5500th year is the time when Christ, God's beloved son is born (see further Chapter 5).

Next we turn to 16.2-3 where the devil flatters the serpent by calling him wiser and greater than all the beasts, and tells him: 'yet you worship the one who is the lesser of you two (so ALCR only). Why do you eat of the weeds of Adam (ALC add: and his wife) and not (AC add: of the fruit) of Paradise?' This, again, called for an explanation, and Arm. and Georg. supplied one, making use of traditions known to them. They tell that Adam used to give nourishment to all the beasts, including the serpent, and that they, therefore, had to worship him every day. (The tradition that Adam and Eve fed the animals in Paradise also occurs in the *Discourse on Abbatôn*. A related tradition, holding that Adam and Eve protected the food in Paradise from the birds and cattle, is found in *Jub.* 3.16; this tradition probably elaborates on Gen. 2.15, where it is said that Adam had to cultivate Paradise and guard it. Feeding the animals, or protecting the crops against animals amplifies the agricultural image suggested in Genesis.) Then Arm. (followed by Georg.) continues: 'You came into being before him; why is it that you, who are the former one, worship the later?' (Compare the story of the jealousy of the devil and his fall in chs. 12–16 of Lat., Arm., Georg.) In this case it is again more likely that the common *Vorlage* of Arm. and Georg. expanded the story than that the archetype of the Greek reduced it to a statement needing further comment.

A last example to be mentioned briefly is ch. 26, which gives God's words to the serpent, corresponding to Gen. 3.14-15. In 26.2-3 the serpent is told that he will lose several parts of his body, all the limbs 'with which you enticed (them) in your depravity'. Arm. (Georg. is somewhat different) adds: 'A likeness of the cross will bring my son to the earth, because of him whom you deceived. Be disabled and broken because of the evil of your heart.'

The Latin Version compared to the Armenian and the Georgian, and to the Greek

The survey of the contents of the Latin version in Chapter 1, pp. 22-24 has shown that, apart from the addition of the account of a vision (or visions) in chs. 25–29, it runs parallel with Arm.–Georg. for chs. 1–44. From that point on, the Latin version differs considerably from all others: Eve's farewell speech is absent, and the story of Adam's and Eve's death and burial is a great deal more compact.

It is highly plausible that the Latin version is the result of a thorough redaction. This is obvious in ch. 44 (Gr. 14). In all versions, except the Latin, that passage relates how Adam commanded Eve to summon their children and tell them how the sin took place. In Lat., however, Eve's account is absent, and Adam commands Eve to tell her sons after his death what she has done; consequently Eve's account is absent here.

The final chapters, concerned with the death and burial of the protoplasts, are also clearly the result of redaction. In the preceding section we noted that Arm. has a large omission here, and that the Slavonic gives these chapters in a thoroughly abbreviated form (as do the Greek manuscripts R and M). In fact, only the Georgian version follows the Greek. The Greek text was clearly felt to be difficult, inconsistent and/or full of redundancies, and various attempts were made to produce a smoother and more coherent account. It should be underlined, however, that the reworkings in Latin, Armenian and RMSlav. differ considerably and do not go back to a common effort to produce a better text.

In chs. 30–44 (Gr. 5–14) the Latin stands nearer to Arm.–Georg. than to the Greek, but it often gives a smoother text. In *GLAE* 7.2 the circumstances of Eve's transgression are clumsily introduced: it is said that when Eve's guardian angels had left her to worship God, the devil gave the forbidden fruit to Eve. Next it is said that the devil knew very well that neither Adam, nor the holy angels were with her. Only then is it said that Eve gave the fruit to Adam. Told in this way, the story raises more questions than it answers. The guardian angels were not yet introduced, and it is not clear why Adam was not with Eve.

Arm.–Georg. follow the Greek text, and then proceed to answer these questions: they explain that Adam and Eve both had their own portions of Paradise to guard (a motif derived from Gr. 15.2-3), and that they both had twelve guardian angels. After these questions are solved, Arm.–Georg. say that because the devil knew that Eve was alone, he had the opportunity to make Eve eat the fruit. The consequence of this interpolated explanation is that it is now said twice that the devil gave Eve from the fruit of the tree. This unevenness is smoothed out in the Latin text, which tells the story in an orderly, logical way: God forbade Adam and Eve to eat from the tree of knowledge; he gave them separate parts of Paradise and two angels each to guard them; when, however, these angels left to worship God, the devil seduced Eve, who ate and gave Adam to eat as well.

A second interesting case is that of the Latin parallel to Gr. 13.3b-5, a passage mentioned already several times before. Here Arm. and Georg. have an explicitly christianized form of the ALCR text in the Greek; the version found in their common ancestor, or a text very similar to it, was known to the author of the Greek *Gospel of Nicodemus* 19 (= *Descensus ad Inferos* 3) where Seth informs the patriarchs and prophets in the underworld about the future resurrection by telling the story of his quest for oil from Paradise. The version found in the Latin *Life of Adam and Eve* agrees verbally with that in the Latin translation of the Greek

Gospel. It is more elaborate than that in Arm.–Georg. or in the Greek *Gospel of Nicodemus.* The question of the relationship between the different versions of the *Gospel of Nicodemus* is complicated (see F. Scheidweiler in W. Schneemelcher, *Neutestamentliche Apokryphen* 1, pp. 395-99; and Nagel, *La vie grecque,* pp. 160-75), but it is clear that among the versions of the *Life of Adam and Eve* the Latin one represents the latest stage in the development of this pericope.

Two further cases may be added that may shed light on the activity of the person(s) responsible for the oldest stage of the *Latin Life of Adam and Eve.* First 22.2 (compare Gr. 1.1). Here the Latin version concludes the part of the text common to Arm., Georg. and Lat. with the sentence 'And the Lord God sent various seeds by the angel Michael and gave them to Adam and showed him how to work and to till the ground so as to have fruit by which they and all their generations might live' (see also Chapter 1, p. 22). This is a convenient ending after all that has been told before. Arm. and Georg. have a similar statement, but at 20.1, immediately after the stories of the quest for food and the penitence of Adam and Eve. This position highlights the connection between penitence and the provision of food, but comes at an awkward place with regard to the flow of the story: Adam is eager to go west to help Eve who is about to give birth to a child. Hence Lat. moved the story about the seeds and the instruction in agriculture to a later and more suitable stage in the narrative.

In yet another instance Latin, while partly agreeing with Arm. and Georg. against the Greek text, goes its own way. In *GLAE* 2–4 the sequence of events is as follows: after Eve has had a horrible dream about Abel and Cain, she and Adam go and look, and find Abel murdered by his brother. Directly after this we are told that God commands Michael to warn Adam not to tell the mystery he knows to Cain, who is a son of wrath. Another son will be given to him and, in fact, Seth is born.

Here Arm.–Georg. give a different story. After Eve's dream Adam and Eve separate the two brothers. Then Adam receives God's message through Michael that he may not relate the mystery he knows to Cain, because he is a son of wrath, but that Seth will be born. Finally, Cain kills Abel (Arm. has here an omission, probably through *homoioteleuton*), and Seth is born.

The Latin version has been edited in a more radical fashion. It mentions the dream, the separation of the brothers and Abel's death, but all very succinctly. Nothing is said about Michael's message to Adam. But as soon as Seth is born, Lat. 25–29 have Adam elaborately describing a vision which he received after his expulsion from Paradise, concluded, in Lat. 29.2, by the remark that Seth should also listen to the 'other mysteries' revealed to Adam since he ate from the tree of knowledge. After this, the manuscripts of groups II–IV add another vision.

The Greek manuscripts R and M and the Slavonic Version

The common Greek ancestor of the Armenian and Georgian versions of the *Life of Adam and Eve* is closely related to the ancestor of the Greek manuscripts ATLC. The same will apply to the Greek text behind the Latin version, although the present Latin text is, also in its oldest form, further removed from ATLC than Arm.–Georg.

The survey of the contents of the Slavonic version in Chapter 1, pp. 24–26 has shown that this version is directly linked to the Greek manuscripts R and M (of the fifteenth and the sixteenth century respective-ly; the Slavonic goes back to the fourteenth century [see Chapter 1, p. 17]). A detailed analysis would show that Slav. is more closely related to M than to R. Jointly and individually, R and M show a number of rather idiosyncratic deviations from the main Greek text. Nagel regarded them as representatives of a special, second form of the Greek text. They clearly belong together, and together they have a special relationship to ATLC. The examples of ATLC-readings given above illustrate this. One should note especially the absence of 13.3b-5 in M Slav.

The Coptic Fragments

Because of the fragmentary state in which they have been transmitted, little can be said about the Coptic versions.

The Berlin fragment (Leipoldt n. 181) seems to agree with the text of the Greek version entirely (disregarding some elaborations to produce a fuller text), except for the last piece, which has a slightly different perspective than its Greek counterpart. In Gr. 29.5-6, God commands the angels (in indirect speech) to allow Adam to take four kinds of fragrance from Paradise; Adam collects them himself. In col. 2 of the *verso* of the Coptic parchment, God commands the angels (in direct speech) to bring the fragrances to Adam. On the basis of this material, however, no conclusions can be drawn about the status of this Coptic text in the history of the writing's transmission. As far as the parts of the text preserved in the Coptic are concerned, all other versions more or less side with the Greek.

In the Manchester fragment (Crum n. 84) a similar situation occurs.

In one or two instances, this text sides with the Armenian against the Greek of 31–32, but these instances are text-critically meaningless (e.g., Gr. 31.4 '*I* do not know how we shall meet...'; Arm. and Copt. '*we* do not know how we shall meet...'). In the final piece of this fragment, containing Eve's confession of sin, the Coptic goes its own way altogether (e.g., Gr. 32.2 and all other versions repeat: 'I have sinned'; Copt. repeats: 'give me repentance'). The transmission of Eve's confession varies widely everywhere, possibly because of liturgical influences. Again, therefore, no conclusions can be drawn about the position of this text in the writing's textual and literary history.

The Earliest Stages of a Complex Tradition Process

The examination of the relationships between the Greek manuscripts and versions in the preceding sections leads to the conclusion that the shortest type of the Greek text, found in DSV (K)PG B, represents the oldest form of the *Life of Adam and Eve* known to us. This conclusion calls, however, for some further comment.

First, it has become clear that the Greek text in this form, gives sometimes such a short version of a story or only a hint at certain traditions, that the reader is left with questions. In the case of Adam's story of the Fall this is so; but here the reader may look forward to the fuller account by Eve in chs. 15–30. Also there, however, the reader would like to have more detailed information, for instance in ch. 16, where Arm. and Georg. promptly supply it. Another instance is 39.1-3 where God says to Adam:

> 'If you had kept my commandment, those who brought you down to this place would not have rejoiced. Yet I tell you that I shall turn their joy into sorrow, but shall turn your sorrow into joy, and I shall establish you in your dominion, and make you sit on the throne of the one who deceived you. But he will be cast into this place to see you sitting above him. Then he will be condemned, and they that listened to him, and he will feel sorrow when he sees you sitting on his throne.'

This presupposes knowledge of the story of the jealousy and fall of the devil that is found in Arm., Georg. (which give a shorter version of ch. 39) and Lat. (which omits this chapter), but is not present in the Greek version known to us.

Does this imply that yet an older Greek version did indeed contain the story of the fall of the devil? It does not. The short form of the Greek text known to us is certainly aware of other traditions concerning Adam and Eve, but that does not necessarily mean that it gives a shorter version of an originally more elaborate text. We have to distinguish between the presence of particular traditions (embodied or presupposed in more than one writing) and the existence of certain documents.

This leads us to another important question: was the lengthy passage at the beginning of the *Life of Adam and Eve* in Arm., Georg. and Lat., but absent in Greek, part of the oldest form of this *Life*, or not?

Let us briefly recapitulate the contents of Lat. chs. 1–21. This passage consists of four episodes: a) Adam and Eve looking for food; b) the penitence of Adam and Eve; c) the devil's account of his own fall; d) the separation of Adam and Eve, and Cain's birth. One thing is clear: either the addition of the four sections at the beginning in Arm. and Georg., followed by Latin, or the omission of them in Greek was deliberate.

The text now found in Arm. and Georg. gives due attention to the penitence of Adam and Eve after their expulsion from Paradise (see also the title of the Armenian version). It shows how at least Adam was victorious in his fight against the devil and it explains, in the story of Satan's fall, how the devil came to hate Adam and Eve. Finally it relates the separation between Eve and Adam and the birth of Cain; and all this before narrating what happened at the death of Adam and Eve, some nine hundred years later.

Arm.–Georg. are therefore richer in content and tend to explain considerably more of what happened than the Greek, which apparently presupposes knowledge of more traditions than the ones contained in it, but does not care to tell them. The question is therefore whether it is more likely that Arm.–Georg. tend to explain what is obscure in the Greek, or whether the Greek is some kind of 'epitome' that has become obscured by its drastic omission of the four opening episodes.

The following observations may help to solve this question.

(1) One should note that there is a certain *inclusio* between the beginning of Arm. and Georg., and the point where they join the Greek in Gr. 1.1. The Armenian version (corresponding largely to Georg.) begins with the words: 'It came to pass, when Adam went forth from the Garden with his wife, outside, to the east of the Garden, they made a hut to live in…' and continues with Adam's and Eve's search for food. After the four episodes are related, Arm. reads: 'Thenceforth Adam took Eve and the child and brought them to the eastern region'. The Greek begins with the same words: 'After they went forth from Paradise,' but immediately continues with the detail

that they went eastwards: 'Adam took Eve and reached the eastern region.' The *inclusio* in Arm. and Georg. (which mentions the travel towards the East twice) may be an indication of a later insertion of the four episodes right in the middle, so to say, of Gr. 1.1.

(2) From here onward Arm. and Georg. (by and large) follow the text of the Greek. The overall presentation of events is perhaps a little awkward: first the story of what happened directly after the expulsion from Paradise, with a flashback concerning the fall of the devil; next Cain's murder of Abel; then what happened at Adam's death and the parting words of Adam and Eve, including two flashbacks (structural elements in farewell discourses) about what happened in the Garden, finally the account of Adam's and Eve's death. Although the text of Arm.–Georg. is fuller and richer in explanation, and more smoothly flowing as a result, the literary composition is considerably weaker than that of the Greek. The Greek is less precise in its presentation of the narrative details, but it is much stricter in form.

(3) The place of the stories of the quest for food and the penitence in RMSlav., immediately after that of the expulsion from the Garden, is more natural than in Arm.-Georg., where they precede the accounts of the fall leading to the expulsion.

Yet neither the place nor the wording of these stories in the common ancestor of RM and Slav. can be original. The textual history of the Greek version tells against this. Also, a particular feature of this extra pericope renders this unlikely. As we have seen in Chapter 1, p. 25, RMSlav. omit any mention of the seeds for food given to Adam when he had to leave Paradise. This, however, is exactly what the stories about the quest for food and the penance in the Jordan and the Tigris are concerned with. Yet RM end with 29.13 'By saying this the devil seduced me a second time, and I went out of the water,' without further reference to the seeds given to Adam (Slav. ends with Eve's victory over the devil).

This state of affairs would seem to favour the following theory: the Greek text found in DSV (K)PG B represents the oldest form of the *Life of Adam and Eve*. Together with it circulated a set of Greek stories about Adam's and Eve's search for food and their penitence (successful in the case of Adam, unsuccessful in that of Eve). These were known to and used by RMSlav. and Arm.–Georg.; Arm.–Georg. also knew further stories about the fall of the devil and the birth of Cain. Whether the latter two episodes were found in the same document as the first two, or whether the four were only brought together at a later stage, we do not know. RMSlav. had more before them than they trans-mitted to their readers, but exactly how much cannot be determined.

The Latin version, finally, can be explained as a further development and thorough redaction of the *Life of Adam and Eve* as represented by Arm.–Georg. It would seem to us that it is not possible to establish whether this development and redaction (or series of redactions?) still took place in the Greek stage of the text's transmission, or whether they form part of the Latin stage.

Further Reading

An earlier attempt to describe the relationships between the versions of the *Life*, not dis-similar to ours, was made by

G.W.E. Nickelsburg, in M.E. Stone (ed.), *Jewish Writings of the Second Temple Period* (CRINT, 2.2; Assen/Philadelphia: Van Gorcum/Fortress, 1984), pp. 110-18.

Other reconstructions are summarized in Stone, *History*, pp. 61-71.

3

CONSTITUTIVE ELEMENTS AND MAIN THEMES IN THE VARIOUS VERSIONS OF THE *LIFE OF ADAM AND EVE*

The *Greek Life of Adam and Eve*

Form

The *Greek Life of Adam and Eve* obviously presupposes the story in Genesis 3, but handles it freely. The basic deviation from the biblical account concerns the form of *GLAE*. Whereas Genesis 3 straight-forwardly tells its story in a chronological order, the story's version in *GLAE* is mainly told in the form of two flashbacks, one by Adam and one by Eve, both given on Adam's deathbed. Moreover, *GLAE* elabo-rately discusses the events surrounding Adam's death and burial, and, more briefly, Eve's death and burial.

This pattern defines *GLAE* as a 'farewell discourse', or, as the form is less aptly called, 'testament'. In this literary form, a man or a woman, usually somebody from the distant past, addresses his or her children when he or she is about to die. When the speech is finished, it is related that the speaker dies and is buried. Numerous Jewish and Christian writings from the Hellenistic and Roman periods respond to this form, the most famous examples being the *Testaments of the Twelve Patriarchs* and the *Assumption of Moses* (on account of its form also erroneously called the *Testament of Moses*).

As to form, the 'farewell discourse' has to contain an introduction, a speech, and an account of the speaker's death and burial. The contents of the speech proper may concern anything, from moral instruction (some virtue or vice being illustrated by events from the speaker's life) to eschatological prophecy (the hour of death being particularly suited for clairvoyant insights). The concluding passage, about the death and burial of the speaker, may be extremely brief (as in the *Testaments of the Twelve Patriarchs*) or rather extended (as, presumably, in the *Assumption of Moses*; see J. Tromp, *The Assumption of Moses* [1993], pp. 270-85). In *GLAE*, this concluding passage is so extensive, that it must be regarded as just as important as the speech (see below).

In two respects *GLAE* differs considerably from other examples of the form. First, it contains two farewell speeches; and the second speech is not delivered by the moribund Adam himself, but vicariously by his wife Eve. The latter of these (chs. 15–30) is undoubtedly the most important one. In the former, spoken by Adam himself (chs. 6–8), the story of the Fall adds hardly anything to the Genesis account except for the introduction of some seventy diseases as a divine punishment. This motif serves as an occasion for Eve's and Seth's quest for medicine against death (9.3–14.2). Their enterprise fails, and when they return empty-handed, Adam despairs and tells Eve to relate to their children how they came to transgress God's commandment (14.3).

Although Adam's speech undoubtedly belongs to the earliest traceable form of *GLAE*, it may well have been absent at yet an earlier stage. Be that as it may, Adam's speech must now be considered as an extension of the introductory passage of the farewell discourse-form. The impending death of the speaker is announced by the words 'he fell ill' (5.2). Adam's subsequent speech explains the origin of illness; the story of Eve's and Seth's quest elaborates that theme, explaining that illness is inescapable. Adam's farewell discourse, together with Eve's and Seth's futile quest thus unmistakably sets the tone for Eve's speech, which climaxes in God's condemnation of humankind to death, and his promise of the eschatological resurrection. Adam's speech can therefore be regarded as part of the extended introduction to the main farewell discourse, the one delivered vicariously by Eve.

This is the second remarkable deviation from the pattern: the farewell discourse is not spoken by the moribund person himself. On the literary level, this is explained by Adam's weakness. He is simply too ill to speak for himself. The effect is that in this way Eve herself takes the responsibility of being seduced in the first place.

Thus, *GLAE* is formally composed as follows. The introduction of the writing, in which the scene for the farewell discourse is set, presents its three main human characters, Adam, Eve and Seth. Adam is the one who is about to die; to signal this, his age and the number of his children are mentioned, as well as the fact that 'he fell ill'. In an excursus, Adam is said to explain the origin of his illness, and Eve and Seth are depicted as attempting (but failing) to procure medicine against his disease to emphasize the inevitability of Adam's death. True to the form, Adam exhorts his children, or rather, has Eve exhort his children. The farewell discourse itself is delivered by Eve.

When Eve has finished speaking, the concluding part of the farewell-form commences (chs. 31–43), the story of Adam's death and burial. This concluding part is extensive, concentrating on Adam's *post mortem* existence. As we shall see below, this part of the writing more or less counterbalances the emphasis on illness and death of Eve's account. The authors go to great lengths to stress that death does not have the last word. In various, often even contradicting ways, the authors want to imprint in the readers' minds that, after his death, Adam lived on in the heavenly Paradise, and that he will be revived in the eschatological future.

Thus, the testament-form most felicitously suits the main theme of *GLAE*, namely, the question of life, death, and afterlife. The flashbacks on Adam's and Eve's transgressions explain why people must die; the events surrounding Adam's death give a prospect on man's heavenly survival and his eschatological resurrection.

Further Reading
On the farewell discourse form, see, for example, the brief introduction by:

H.W. Hollander, 'The Testaments of the Twelve Patriarchs', in M. de Jonge (ed.), *Outside the Old Testament* (Cambridge: Cambridge University Press, 1985), pp. 71-91,

or the extensive studies by:

E. Cortès, *Los discursos de adiós des Gn 49 a Jn 13-17: Pistas para la historia de un género literario en la antigua judía* (Barcelona: Herder, 1976).

E. von Nordheim, *Die Lehre der Alten* I-II (Leiden: Brill, 1980–85).

'Rewriting the Bible'
The above observations about the form of *GLAE* have shown that this writing differs from Genesis 3 in several respects. In this section, we shall discuss the relationship of *GLAE* to Genesis 3 as regards contents.

First of all, conspicuous exegetical decisions underly the story of the Fall according to *GLAE*. A number of details may here be cited. *GLAE* agrees with broad interpretative traditions in establishing a close connection between the serpent and the devil. No such connection exists in Genesis 3, where diabolical figures are entirely absent. However, from the Hellenistic period onwards, it is almost generally accepted that the devil played an important role. In Rev. 12.9 and 20.2, for instance, the devil is simply identified with 'that ancient serpent'. Another example concerns the nakedness of Adam and Eve. To judge from the works of Philo and from patristic exegesis, it was an ancient question what could be meant by the remark in Gen. 3.7 that the eyes of Adam and Eve 'were opened, and they recognized that they were naked'. To the ancient interpreters, it was inconceivable that Adam and Eve, when they were created, were physically blind (see, e.g., Philo, *Quaest. in Gen.* 1.39). An often proposed solution, also followed in *GLAE*, was to take their blindness metaphorically, and their nakedness as the 'denudation' from glory (the 'fall'; see S.P. Brock, 'Jewish Traditions in Syriac Sources' [1979], pp. 221-23). Finally, a more incisive explanation concerns the question how it was possible that Eve was seduced. Again, *GLAE* is in unison with broad streams in Jewish and Christian interpretations of the Fall by claiming that Eve was alone, unguarded by her husband or the angels (for instance, *Protevangelium of James* 13.1; see, for a discussion of this motif in the rabbinical literature, M. Poorthuis, 'Sexisme als zondeval').

Other details should not be understood as answers to interpretative problems, but simply as elaborations motivated by the desire of embellishment. Thus, Paradise is pictured as surrounded by a wall with doors (17.1; 19.1); and when God comes to Paradise to judge Adam, he is seated on a chariot and preceded by trumpet-blowing angels (22.1-3).

It is important to stress that these and other embellishments, as well as the minor interpretative elements are probably not the invention of the authors of *GLAE*, but part and parcel of the stories about the fall of the protoplasts as they knew it. This is particularly clear in the casual and inconsistent way in which many of the extras *vis-à-vis* the Genesis account are presented. For instance, in 17.1-2 it is said that the devil, in order to mislead Eve, was disguised as an angel. In the very next sentence he is depicted as hanging from the wall of Paradise (therefore in the form of the serpent), whereas Eve saw him in the likeness of an angel. A grave inconsistency like this is conceivable only if we accept that the authors were not much interested in the exact detail. Only if they were acquainted (not by reading Genesis, but by hearing the story as it was traditionally told) both with the tradition that the devil could disguise himself as an angel, and with the tradition that he spoke through the mouth of the serpent, could they have had no problem in combining these details. This means that, at least as far as details such as these are concerned, their main interest in composing this writing was not exegetical. Instead, the interpretative elements were already present in the stories as they knew it.

So if we say that *GLAE* presupposes Genesis 3, that statement must be understood to mean that its authors took the story of Adam and Eve, including the interpretations of details and the embellishments, as their starting-point. This statement remains true, even if they perused Genesis 3 (again) before writing their story (which is by no means evident)—the traditional exegesis would then automatically have crept into their reading of Genesis (in the very same way in which Christians automatically read the eschatological parts of *GLAE* in the light of Christ and reformulated accordingly; see below, Chapter 4, pp. 67-75).

We hold, then, that the intention of the authors of GLAE was not to interpret the biblical account, and it follows that it was not their intention just to tell the story of the Fall of Adam and Eve either. They tell the story of the origin of death, because it is the perfect contrast to the main theme: immortality and resurrection. Eve's speech about the origin of death (which is inescapable in this world), and the story of Adam's death and burial (being the story of his heavenly survival and of the promise of the eschatological resurrection) form a diptych, in which the diabolically inspired, fatal destiny of all people is contrasted with the hope on the gracious God who may once lead them into Paradise, after all.

The reason for writing *GLAE* was not to explain the Genesis-account, nor to improve upon it, but to convey the comforting message that life in this valley of tears is not at all without prospect. The first humans fell from glory and were expelled from Paradise; also, the way back into Paradise is closed for the time of our lives. But this miserable life does not end in the inexorable death. God is gracious, and the survival of Adam in the heavenly Paradise, as well as the promise of his future resurrection are as much an example for humankind as his transgression, condemnation and death.

Further Reading

A critical account of the use of the term 'rewritten bible' to denote a particular genre can be found in:

J. Tromp, 'Literary and Exegetical Issues in the Story of Adam's Death and Burial (GLAE 31-42)', in. J. Frishman and L. Van Rompay (eds.), *The Book of Genesis in Jewish and Oriental Christian Interpretation* (Traditio Exegetica Graeca, 5; Louvain: Peeters, 1997).

Main themes

As stated above, the *Greek Life of Adam and Eve* is essentially a writing about the question of life, death and afterlife. We shall now describe in a more or less systematic way the main themes of *GLAE*, how they are treated and how they are related to each other.

(a) Illness and death. The first half of the document (esp. chs. 5–30) mainly deals with the necessity of death. Since the fall of Adam and Eve, people have no longer access to the tree of life (28.3). Instead, Adam was punished with every conceivable disease (some 70 diseases in total, 8.2), and thus irrevocably bound to death. The medical standards of the time should be remembered here. If, in ancient writings, someone is said to 'fall ill', the implication is practically always that he or she is about to die (so also in 5.2). Every disease is potentially fatal, and if humankind is punished with 70 diseases, it is clear that there is no escape from death. Moreover, this world does not produce medicine against death, as Seth and Eve discovered. They went to Paradise to ask for 'oil from the tree of mercy', which apparently would have given health and life back to Adam (9.3), but it was refused to them (13.5). So the point seems to be that there is no escape from death in this world. When Seth and Eve return to Adam with empty hands, Adam cries out that since Eve's fall, 'death is master of the entire human race' (14.2).

If death is merciless, this earthly life does not know grace either (27.3-4). In Eve's account of the Fall, the first humans are presented as consciously disobedient to God (18.2; 21.4; cf. 16.4), and consequently deprived of their original glory (20.1-2; 21.5-6). Exiled from Paradise, man has to live in hard labour, fruitlessly tilling the unfriendly soil; his life will be bitter and devoid of pleasures (24.2-3). Even the animals, who were formerly subjugated to Adam, will rise against him (24.4; cf. 10-12). Man's wife will suffer intolerable pains when giving birth to her children; although she will never again swear to give in to the carnal sin, she will return to her husband (25.1-4; the concept of 'carnal sin', i.e., sexual lust and indulgence, is only mentioned in passing here, and is not discussed as such; cf. G.A. Anderson, 'Celibacy or Consummation in the Garden?' [1989]).

Compared with this life, death itself can be a welcome companion. When Adam is about to die, Eve is horrified at the prospect of having to live on her own; but Adam tells her not to worry, for she will soon die as well (31.2-3).

However, hope shines through in this dismal existence. To those who behave properly outside Paradise, the resurrection is promised, and the fruit of the tree of life will be given to them, so that they may be immortal forever (28.4; in manuscripts ALCR, this promise is

recorded already in 13.3-5). Eve's account of the fall is therefore concluded with the warning not to depart from virtue (30). Immortality
and the resurrection at the end of time are the main subjects of the second half of the writing.

(b) Immortality and resurrection. After God has negated mercy to
Adam, he is said to promise him the resurrection and eternal life. 'If you
guard yourself from every evil, even as to prefer death (namely, above
doing evil), I shall raise you again when the resurrection has come, and
you will be given from the tree of life and you shall be immortal until
eternity' (28.4; in 41.3 it is made clear that Adam's resurrection will be
part of the resurrection of all humankind). Again, when God bewails
Adam, he promises to Adam that he will turn his sadness into joy, and
restore him to his original glory, making him sit on the throne of his
adversary (39.2-3). The eschaton is therefore understood to bring the
perfect restoration of the paradisiac existence for Adam and all
humankind, even a better existence than Adam used to have, because he
will be given from the tree of life and live eternally; moreover, the devil
and his followers will be condemned, and will no longer trouble him
(39.3; in passing, it may be noted that in *GLAE* 24-26, Adam, Eve and
the serpent are condemned, but the devil is not; on the contrary, the
enmity between the devil and humankind is one of the central elements
in the human predicament; see below).

This promise of the eschatological restoration to glory does not post-
pone the divine grace to the end of times. Immediately after Adam's
death, the angels and the sun and the moon offer incenses and prayers to
God, that he may have mercy on Adam (33.4–36.1). Their efforts succeed, and trumpets announce the favourable outcome of God's gracious
verdict on Adam (37.1-2). A Seraph washes Adam in the Acherusian
lake (37.3), a ritual known from Greek mythology as the *post mortem*
cleansing from guilt of the dead. Then God hands him over to Michael,
who is to bring Adam to the third heaven, where he is to remain until
the day of visitation (37.4-6).

It would be erroneous to try to harmonize this view of afterlife with
the concept of the eschatological resurrection. It is tempting to distinguish between a bodily resurrection and the survival of the soul in some
heavenly Paradise immediately after death. *GLAE*, however, does not
make the distinction, but gives every impression that Adam's assumption
into heaven is as bodily as his resurrection. Nevertheless, it is made
abundantly clear that Adam is really dead. Chs. 38–41 extensively

describe Adam's burial in the region of Paradise. This perhaps somewhat naive combination of what seem to us incompatible views on afterlife is not unique. It may very well be that the dead, even the corpses themselves, were not seen as definitively without consciousness as it would seem to many modern readers. One moment before Adam's grave is sealed, his dead body is still capable of responding to God (41.1-2). Possibly, the well-known ancient euphemism for death, 'to sleep', was meant less metaphorically than as our own world-view would understand it.

In any event it is clear that Adam's death is not seen as the final event of his life. It is a stage of his existence, less conscious perhaps than his past life or his life in the eschatological future, but not a state of non-existence. The authors of *GLAE* do not consistently distinguish between body and soul. They are familiar with both aspects of human life, but appear indifferent with regard to the exact relationship between them. They are aware that body and soul (or spirit) can be separated, but do not strictly separate them conceptually. A similar lack of interest as far as consistency is concerned is evident in the way *GLAE* handles the location of Paradise. Adam's body is buried near the earthly Paradise, and he is taken up to Paradise in the third heaven; but there is no indication whatsoever that the authors distinguished between both Paradises (see on this matter in detail J. Tromp, 'Literary and Exegetical Issues').

Minor themes

(a) Guilt. Next to underlining the inescapability of death in this world, the *Greek Life of Adam and Eve* also discusses the cause of death, which it obviously seeks in the story of the Fall.

Every contemplation of the story of the Fall leads to the conclusion that the history of humankind began with an intricate tragedy of crime and punishment. Theological speculation and exegesis go hand in hand trying to expose the truly blameworthy ones, and to exculpate God, the one who is, after all, seen as the author of this world *and* its history. Already in the Genesis account, the authors waveringly shift the main culpability from Adam to Eve and the serpent. In later accounts, the devil is introduced, resulting only, it seems, in complicating matters further. This figure moves attention away from God, but still everybody feels that there is something reasonable in his refusal to worship Adam. Few theologians have been as successful in excusing God as Ephraem Syrus (c. 306–373), who in his commentary on Genesis wrote:

God wanted to give them the eternal life on account of their righteousness. So he gave them a command. That command, however, was not heavy, compared to the great reward that was prepared for them. On the contrary, he prohibited them one single tree—just enough to be able to speak of a command. On the other hand, he gave them the entire Paradise, so that they would in no way be forced to transgress the law (see R.-M. Tonneau [ed.], *Sancti Ephraem Syri in Genesim* [1955], p. 30; our translation follows the Dutch translation by Janson and Van Rompay, *Efrem de Syriër* [1993]).

In the *Greek Life of Adam and Eve*, there is no such sophisticated solution to the problem. All characters featuring in the story are more or less guilty, except God.

God is, by definition, without fault. However, his creatures sometimes have to be reminded of this basic fact. When the angels cease chasing Adam from Paradise, the Lord angrily asks them. 'Why have you stopped expelling Adam? Was it I who sinned, or was my judgment wrong?' The angels immediately confess that the Lord is righteous and that he has judged justly (27.4-5).

The assessment of Adam's and Eve's guilt in *GLAE* is a complicated matter. Both of them are guilty, as well as the serpent, that much is clear. Adam is condemned for transgressing the commandment and listening to his wife (24.1; cf. 39.1); Eve is condemned for listening to the serpent and transgressing the commandment (25.1); the serpent, finally, is condemned for being prepared to act as a disgraceful instrument, that is, as an instrument of Satan (26.1; cf. 16.5).

Their blameworthiness is stressed by a phrase expressing that they were all perfectly aware of the forbidden nature of their actions. Before giving in to their respective seducers, they hesitate and say 'I am afraid that God might be angry with me' (16.4; 18.2; 21.4).

On the other hand, the story seems to adduce attenuating circumstances for both Adam and Eve. As a woman, Eve is essentially weak. The devil was able to seduce her, because she was alone, unguarded by either her husband or the angels (7.1-2; 17.1-2; cf. 29.7-13 in manuscripts R and M). The implication of this remark must be that women who are left on their own are especially liable to seduction, probably by nature.

In fact, Eve goes to great lengths in taking all the blame. When Adam has fallen ill, we are told that she wished that she might bear half of his pain, 'because this has happened to you on my account' (9.2; cf. 10.2; 11.1-2; 14.2), and when she prays for mercy on Adam, she unremittingly echoes the phrase 'I have sinned', concluding only by saying 'and all sins in the creation have come about through me' (32.2;

contrast, however, Adam's confession in 27.2 that 'I alone have sinned').

Thus, the inescapable impression is that the Fall is essentially a tragic accident. Adam is said to blame Eve. It is through her that he will die (14.2), a fact that Eve is said to acknowledge readily. At the same time, however, Adam excuses her. She was seduced when she was left unguarded (7.1-2), and therefore could not help it (the question whether Adam might have been able to resist his wife's temptation is not raised).

If we would ask who, according to the authors of *GLAE* was more to blame, Adam or Eve, we receive no answer from the writing. As often, the authors do not attempt to present clear-cut ideas about various motifs in their story. Apparently, the question of guilt and the relationship between the sexes was not of primary interest to them.

(b) Enmity between humankind, the devil, and the animal world. The character of Eve is comparable to that of the serpent. Both are instruments of the devil (16.5; 21.3), who uses them to reach his eventual goal: to have Adam evicted from Paradise (16.3). In this sense, *GLAE* is also the story of Satan's enmity against humankind (28.4). Consequently, 'the enemy' is the most appropriate designation for the devil (2.4; 7.2; 15.1; 25.4; 28.4; cf. 'deceiver' 39.2).

Subordinate to this enmity of more cosmic dimensions, there is the enmity between humankind and the animal world (cf. 26.4). This may be the subject of the curious episode in which Seth is attacked by an animal (see on this passage G.A. Anderson, 'The Penitence Narrative in the *Life of Adam and Eve*', pp. 29-33). When Eve rebukes the animal for its behaviour, it reciprocates the accusation. Seth, however, with a single, stern word causes the animal to retreat 'until the day of judgment' (chs. 10–12). The gist of this story escapes us. Could it be that it is meant as some kind of aetiological explanation of the domestication of animals by man? This may be indicated especially by the beast's remark that, since Eve's transgression, the nature of the animals has 'changed' (11.2).

(c) Grace and Salvation. Proper conduct and a humble service to the Lord are the conditions which are to be met if God is eventually to show his mercy to his human creatures. *GLAE* does not reckon with a perfectly saintly life; if anywhere, the writing's concern with common people is expressed in Adam's last words to Eve. 'Go, pray for me, for we do not know how we will meet our Maker, whether he will have mercy on us, or be wroth with us' (31.4).

'Act properly,' Eve advises her children (30.1). What proper behaviour is, however, how exactly we should act to avoid God's ire, is not discussed. In *GLAE* the essentially imperfect morality of humans is presupposed. It describes the human existence as a tragedy, ridden with explicable, but nonetheless imputable guilt. Humans are beings who, because of their disobedience, have lost the glory originally vested in them. They may regain that glory in the life beyond, if they act properly and are mercifully accepted by God. Acting properly means avoiding transgression of God's commandments; it is apparently taken for granted that the commandments themselves are known.

GLAE does not seem to be far off from the teaching of original sin that has been so popular with Augustine and in the reformed churches. The universality of human sinfulness (corresponding with the universality of death and with the universality of the eschatological resurrection; see 41.3) is also known from early Christian writings. In Romans 5.12-21 the universal sinfulness and death, brought about by the transgression of one man, is contrasted to the gracious salvation, equally brought about by one man, Jesus Christ. It should be noted, however, that in *GLAE*, apart from good conduct and humble prayer for mercy, no factors that might move God to mercy are brought forward, except his sovereign will. Only if God wills, individuals will receive eternal, blissful life. This distinguishes the earliest traceable version of the *Life of Adam and Eve* from its successive stages. No attention whatsoever is paid to Jesus Christ's salvific mediation. This conspicuous absence of the Adam–Christ antithesis pressingly urges the question about the milieu in which *GLAE* originated. Was it Christian or Jewish? Or, in other words, is a Christian *Life of Adam and Eve* without Christ's relief of the Adamic order conceivable? We shall discuss this question in chapter 4.

The Armenian–Georgian *Life of Adam and Eve*

Very little has been written on the theme to be treated in this section. In the past the attention of scholars centered around the problem of the relationship between *GLAE* and *LLAE* and on the specific elements and themes of either of these versions. However, our analysis in chapter 2 has shown that we cannot properly deal with the characteristics of the Latin version before discussing those of the *Vorlage* of the Armenian

and the Georgian. Because of the fact that these have only been published relatively recently, they have not yet been studied closely. More
detailed research will be needed before definitive conclusions about the
Tendenz of the document behind Arm.–Georg. can be reached.

In the meantime we may try to take up a number of issues referred
to earlier (in Chapter 1, pp. 20-22 and in Chapter 2, pp. 35-37 and 42-
43). First of all we have to pay attention to the presence of the equivalent of Lat. chs. 1–21 at the beginning of the *Vorlage* of Arm.–Georg.
What are the main themes, and how does the addition of these chapters
affect the presentation of the themes found in the Greek and in
Arm.–Georg. and the overall constitution of the document?

In his study 'The Penitence Narrative in the *Life of Adam and Eve*',
G.A. Anderson (taking up some points made earlier by M.E. Stone) has
given a penetrating analysis of chs. 1–21 in Arm.–Georg. and Latin. He
has shown that in Arm.–Georg. there exists a very close relationship
between Adam and Eve's search for appropriate food after their expulsion from Paradise and their penitence. Anderson finds here an attempt
to give an interpretation of Gen. 3.17b-19 in connection with Gen.
1.29-30. The following story, about Eve's severe pains when she is
about to give birth to Cain, can be connected with Gen. 3.16. Only
the section about the fall of Satan stands on its own and forms a more
or less unexpected intermezzo in 11.2–17.2.

Anderson posits an 'origin of the major thematic concerns of the
penitence narrative in a close reading of the Biblical text' and shows
that many of the exegetical features found here have parallels in well-
known Jewish traditions (p. 37). He may be right, although it is doubt-
ful that the authors of the earliest form of the stories found in the
chapters concerned—with or (earlier) without the story of Satan's
fall—were still aware of the exegetical roots of the traditions they
incorporated (see also pp. 47-49).

In any case, the search for food and the penitence are closely connected, particularly in Arm.–Georg., giving the earliest version of these
chapters known to us. Adam and Eve can no longer enjoy the angelic
food of Paradise, and outside the Garden they only find 'the grass of the
field', which was suitable as food for animals only (2.1; 3.1, 3. 4.1-3).
They decide to do penance in the hope of receiving proper food (6.2;
8.2). This is granted to Adam immediately after he has completed his
penance (20.1); he receives seeds and instructions on how to sow and to
reap. Eve, who fails in her penitence, has in the meantime gone to the
west, where she will give birth to Cain. She describes her situation as

follows. 'Behold I shall go to the west and I shall be there and my food (will be) grass until I die; for henceforth I am unworthy of the foods of life' (18.1 in Arm., cf. Georg.).

Also in the Latin version and in the extract found in the Greek manuscripts R and M (29.7-13) the penitence is undertaken because of the lack of food, but it seems to serve the wider purpose of placating God's wrath and re-establishing good relations between God and the protoplasts. R and M do not mention that Adam received seeds and learns how to use them (at this point the Slavonic version, related to these two Greek manuscripts, is very different), and the Latin mentions this theme only later, at a more suitable place in the narrative (22.2; see Chapter 2, p. 39).

Anderson has drawn attention to yet another feature of the penitence story, that can also be found in the subsequent section on Eve's birth-pains. In chapters 1–21 Adam's culpability is minimized. In 3.2 (cf. 5.3) Eve takes all the blame; Adam's reaction 'Great wrath has come upon us, I know not whether because of you or because of me' can hardly be called a firm denial. There is a great difference between Adam's stay in the Jordan and that of Eve in the Tigris. Adam is surrounded like a wall by all beings living in the water (Arm.) or even living on the borders of the Jordan (Georg.), and the flow of the water is stopped (ch. 8). Eve stands on a stone, with waters reaching up to her neck (chs. 6–7). Adam succeeds whereas Eve fails; she not only sinned against God's commandment, but also disobeyed Adam's instructions concerning the penance in the river (6.1; 7.1; 10.3; 18.1, cf. 21.3b). In the following story it is thanks to Adam's intercession on behalf of Eve that help from heaven enables Eve to survive Cain's birth (chs. 20–21, see in particular 21.2).

To what extent did this approach to the events in the life of Adam and Eve after their expulsion affect the presentation in Arm.–Georg. of the joint material with the Greek? The answer must be that there are remarkably few alterations with regard to the main themes and the constitutive elements.

The important passage Gen. 3.8-19, dealing with God's punishment of Adam, Eve and the serpent, lies at the basis of the narrative in chs. 22–29 in Gr. Arm. and Georg. There is no direct relationship between this section and the treatment of important elements of the same passage from Scripture in the stories just discussed above. Arm.–Georg. omits, however, the reference to the seeds given to Adam by God in 29.5-6. Earlier, in the passage corresponding to Gr. chs. 1–5 Arm.–Georg.

omits all references to the birth of Cain which it has already recorded before.

As to the apportioning of blame to Eve rather than to Adam we may point to the longer text in Arm.–Georg. of ch. 7 (Arm.–Georg. 32–33) that stresses Adam's ignorance. 'Eve caused me, who did not know, to eat of it' (Arm. 32.3); 'et elle me séduisit, mes fils, car je ne savais pas' (Georg., repeating the statement in 33.3). Later, in the version of the same event found in Eve's testament, Georg. 44 (corresponding to Gr. 21; Arm. 44 is much shorter here) makes Eve tell Adam that she will take full responsibility in case God asks him what has happened. There is no equivalent of Adam's complaint in Gr. 21.6 'O, wicked woman, what have you wrought among us. You have estranged me from the glory of God,' but a nearly identical phrase in 14.2 is not left out. Also in other instances, including those in the final section, chs. 31–43, of the *Life of Adam and Eve* there are no signifcant differences between Arm.–Georg. and Greek in statements concerning the guilt of Adam and Eve. Those responsable for the *Vorlage* of the Armenian and Georgian versions clearly did not aim at bringing all passages concerned with this important topic in line; in this they followed the lead of the Greek version (see pp. 53–54).

Finally, some remarks on the clarifying additions in Arm.–Georg., briefly discussed in Chapter 2, pp. 36–37, are in order. One point in the longer text of chapter 7 has just been noted. In 16.2-3 Arm.–Georg. explains the very brief reference to the fall of Satan in the Greek; but there is no explicit link to the story told earlier at some length. A similar reference to this story is found in Gr. ch. 39; Arm.–Georg. has here a shorter version (see Chapter 2, p. 41), but this is to avoid duplication.

The clearly Christian passages in 13.3-5 and 26.3 (and that in 27.5-6 in Georg.) do not affect the structure and the overall message of the document. For Christians God's future intervention on behalf of Adam and his offspring included, of necessity, the coming and activity of Jesus Christ. In the case of the Armenian and Georgian versions of the *Life of Adam and Eve* Jesus Christ is only mentioned, so to speak, in the margin.

The Latin *Vita Adae et Evae*

As we have seen in the previous chapters (see Chapter 1, pp. 22-24 and Chapter 2, pp. 37-40) *LLAE* differs considerably from any of the other versions. If we compare it to Arm.–Georg. to which it is nearest, we note a) two additions (chs. 25–29 with Adam's vision[s] narrated to Seth, and chs. 49–50 with Eve's parting words and her instructions to make tablets on which the events contained in this book can be written), b) a significant omission (Gr. chs. 15–30: Eve's account of the Fall and the expulsion from Paradise) and c) a considerably shorter version of Adam's departure from the earth (chs. 45–48). Earlier we have also noted that in those passages where the Latin runs parallel to one or more of the others it gives, in general, a smoother and more consistent text. The result of these drastic editorial activities is a writing very different in form and content from the other ones. (Our analysis limits itself to the shorter version found in Meyer's group I; but the same is *a fortiori* true of the Latin text found in the other groups of manuscripts.)

As to form, *LLAE* is a story about significant events in the life of Adam and Eve, including a number of flashbacks. We find only some remnants of the farewell discourse form (chs. 28–41 and 49–50).

The present text can be divided into two parts, of nearly equal length. First there are the episodes of the search for food, the penitence (with the story of the fall of Satan), Eve's pains and the birth of Cain, the birth of Abel and his death, the birth of Seth and other children, taking up chs. 1–24. Adam's account to Seth of his vision (chs. 25–29) concludes this part.

The second part deals with the events before and after Adam's death. It records Adam's account of the Fall, Eve's and Seth's quest for the oil from Paradise ending with a refusal and Michael's promise of what will happen when God's beloved Son Christ will come on earth (chs. 30–43). Adam commands Eve to tell their children what she has done to bring transgression, sin and death upon all generations, and he dies (chs. 44–45). Seth (in 48.6 unexpectedly joined by Eve) is allowed to see how God has mercy on his creature, and now hands him over to Michael to guard him until the day of dispensing punishment in the last years; then he will sit on the throne of Satan who deceived him. Adam is buried in Paradise, together with Abel (chs. 46–48). Next, Eve's farewell words and instructions concerning the tablets follow in chs. 49–50, and ch. 51 records her death and burial.

As to the main themes, like the other versions the *Latin Life of Adam and Eve* is interested in the human plight and the final destiny of human beings. Adam is clearly the central figure; he is the true penitent and receives God's mercy—as is shown to Seth after his death, and will become evident to all on the last day. He has sinned, but Eve was the first to transgress God's commands and she also succumbed to the temptation of Satan yet a second time. Time and again she recognizes her responsibility and confesses her guilt. (On this see particularly John R. Levison, *Portraits of Adam in Early Judaism* [1988], pp. 174-85.) Seth, who is an important figure in the other versions too, gets a very prominent role in the *LLAE*. He is Adam's most favourite son who not only, with Eve, tries to get oil from Paradise for Adam, but also receives important and essential information, in chs. 25–29, 37–40 and 47–48. He is the figure who is eminently suited to make the tablets ordered by Eve (51.3, following ch. 50).

The account in chs. 1–21, beginning with the search for food and ending with the birth of Cain is by and large the same in Latin as in Arm.–Georg. but, as we have seen in section 2 above, with regard to the penitence the emphasis is not so much on the lack of food as on the need for God's pity and mercy in general. Adam takes the initiative for the penance in the Jordan and the Tigris, is (still) able to exercise dominion on the animal world and to stop the water of Jordan (ch. 8), and he persists in his penitence completing his forty days in the Jordan successfully (ch. 17). Eve wanders westward after being deceived a second time, to stay there until she dies (ch. 18). When in her birth-pains she calls to God for mercy, she does not receive it; only because of Adam's intercession does she get the help from heaven she urgently needs (chs. 19–21). Later Adam tells Seth (chs. 25–28) that after the expulsion from Paradise he was taken up to the 'Paradise of righteousness' in heaven. God told him that he would die 'because you have transgressed the commandment of God, since you have listened rather to the voice of your wife, whom I gave in your power, that you might control her. But you listened to her and transgressed my words' (26.3). At this occasion Adam pleaded for mercy; the Latin of the Lord's answer is difficult to translate; so much is clear, however, that there will always be descendants of Adam to serve God; he was after all created with love of knowledge. (The account of another vision concerning the future must have followed here, but what it contained is not certain—see Chapter 1, p. 23.)

In the second part Adam, about to die, tells his children what happened in Paradise. Eve ate of the forbidden tree; 'she ate of it herself and gave the same to me' (33.3). Adam is held responsible by God and punished with 70 plagues. Hence he is now dying in great pain and asks for the oil of life from the tree of mercy in Paradise (chs. 34–35). Eve is very much distressed and confesses her sin (35.2). After Eve's and Seth's mission to procure the oil, it is Adam who reproaches Eve. 'A great plague have you brought upon us, transgression and sin for all our generations.' Therefore she has to tell her children what she did—so that they and their descendants will understand why they have to lead such difficult lives (ch. 44). This is what she does (very briefly) in chs. 49–50 telling 'what the archangel Michael said to us when your father and I (sic) transgressed the command of God'. When Adam dies Eve stares 'at the ground with her hands folded over her head, and all her children weep bitterly' (46.2). It is Seth who hears the promises concerning Adam; Eve joins him in watching the burial of Adam and Abel (48.6).

Summing up: although parallels can be found in the other versions for many individual utterances of Adam and Eve, and for statements concerning their respective responsibilities, *LLAE*, unlike the other versions, seem to be concerned primarily with the questions of guilt and penitence. The overall picture of the protoplasts is clearly biased. Adam's culpability is minimized, Eve's guilt receives much emphasis.

Among the passages in which Seth plays a role, the treatment of the episode of the beast in the story of the quest for oil (chs. 37–39 = Gr. 10–12) calls for some comment. The beast that attacks Seth is not just a wild animal, no longer subject to humans because of Eve's transgression (see also Gr. 24.4), but the serpent which bites Seth (37.1; 39.2 and 44.1; cf. Gen. 3.15). There is a continuous enmity between Satan and humankind and Seth recognizes that. He says to the beast. 'May the Lord God rebuke you! Be silent, be dumb, shut your mouth, accursed enemy of truth, confounder and destroyer. Stand back from the image of God until the day when the Lord God orders you to be brought to trial' (39.1). The serpent obeys him. For the Latin version there is a connection between chs. 11–17, 33.2, chs. 37–39 and 48.3.

The Slavonic *Life of Adam and Eve*

The editors of the Slavonic version have, through radical omissions and a number of additions, drastically changed the tendency of the *Life of Adam and Eve*. Attention has been moved away from the theme of death and immortality, and the writing is mainly focused on the sustenance motif.

Formally, the Slavonic version retains the pattern of the Greek version. The introduction is followed by the story of Cain, Abel, and Seth; also present are Adam's farewell discourse and Eve's and Seth's quest for the oil from the tree of life. There are no formal deviations in Eve's account and the stories of Adam's and Eve's deaths and burials, either.

Regarding the contents, great differences exist. As was already remarked in Chapter 1, Slav. agrees with the Greek manuscripts R and M in omitting many details from the Greek recension. Such differences must essentially be ascribed to the textual development of the writing. They were absent already from the common ancestor of Slav. and RM. Manuscripts R and M probably represent this text-form more or less as such. The text offered in those manuscripts is meagre, but its structure and tendency are essentially unaltered.

However, the editors of the Slavonic recension have filled the skeletal story before them with traditions not present in the earlier forms of the writing, especially traditions concerning the question what Adam and Eve had to eat outside Paradise.

This question has an important place in the *Slavonic Life of Adam and Eve*. Several passages are adapted to meet the new theme of the writing. The introduction has been changed. It says that Adam was master of all animals and decided what and when these animals could eat (1). Further on in the story, Eve reprimands the animal that attacks Seth by reminding it of the way she used to feed it with her own hands; but the animal (that is called Kotur) retorts that Eve no longer has power over them through her transgression, but that Kotur himself will feed on her and her children (10.3–11.2; Turdeanu ['La *Vie d'Adam et d'Eve*', p. 76] suggests that the name Kotur for the animal originated from textual corruption). When Adam is being chased from Paradise, he asks the angels to allow him to pray to God, not for the fruit from the tree of life (28.2), but for food for their sustenance, and fragrances. Adam apparently does not receive food (as in manuscripts R and M, the mention of the seeds is absent), but he does receive the fragrances to offer to God.

The central focus of the story then is on Adam's and Eve's repentance, motivated by their hunger (29.7-9). The question what they should eat is answered by the command to work on the land and to tame animals, especially oxen, to plow the soil (Slav. chs. 30–32; the command is phrased with the words of Adam's condemnation [cf. Gen. 3.17-19], which is absent in the counterpart to Gr. 27.2). Adam receives one seventh of paradise to till, and when he is plowing the earth, the devil persuades him to sign a contract (the so-called *cheirographon*) in which Adam subdues himself to the devil as to the master of earthly matters. In an aside, it is said that Adam did so knowingly, acknowledging the real Lord, and knowing that this Lord would come to earth in human form and subdue the devil. Next, Adam and Eve repent, and, although the devil attempted to seduce Eve anew, they both are successful (29.10-13; Slav. chs. 35–39). Although it is not stated explicitly, the outcome of their repentance must be the annulment of the diabolic contract through Jesus Christ. In what follows, the stories of Adam's and Eve's death and burial are only related very briefly (as in the Greek manuscripts R and M).

Turdeanu ('La *Vie d'Adam et d'Eve*', pp. 115-22) has convincingly argued that the story of the *cheirographon* originated fairly late (Turdeanu suggests in Bulgaria) as the combination and folkloristic elaboration of several scriptural facts, namely the command to till the earth (Gen. 3.23), the devil's dominion over the earth (e.g., Jn 12.31 and 2 Cor. 4.4), and Christ's nullification of the document containing incriminating evidence against humanity, and his victory over the powers of this world (Col. 2.14-15).

The success of Adam's and especially Eve's repentance is remarkable. It is she who proposes to repent and who voluntarily suggests that she would fast for a longer period than Adam. In this respect, the Slavonic deviates from all other text forms, including the text form of the Greek manuscripts R and M (Georg. 5.3-6.1 is only superficially similar). In that form, as represented by manuscript R, Adam takes the initiative and tells Eve to fast for 40 days; he himself will fast for 44 days. In Slav., however, the state of affairs is exactly the reverse. This editorial change must have been deliberate, and can be explained by the great importance attached to the protoplasts' repentance in the Slavonic tradition, where Adam's prayer for mercy is often explicitly addressed to the Lord Jesus—a prayer which, in the Christian view, cannot but be successful (see Turdeanu, 'La *Vie d'Adam et d'Eve*', pp. 122-41).

Summing up: the theme of immortality (or, more dominantly in this version, resurrection) is certainly present in the Slavonic version. One receives the impression, however, that the Slavonic editors, when fleshing out the skeleton of their *Vorlage*, gave the entire writing a new direction, resulting in a kind of aetiological legend of agriculture as the poor substitute for paradisiac food.

This new form of the *Life* attracted new traditions and produced new details. The traditio-historical study of these new elements clearly shows that the Slavonic *Life* is in all respects essentially Christian, comparable to such Byzantine chronicles as the *Palaea* (dating to the ninth century and extant in later Slavonic versions into which the *Life* is often incorporated; see Turdeanu, 'La *Vie d'Adam et d'Eve*', p. 114), retelling the Old Testament as part of the one, integrated Christian Bible.

Further Reading

The main exegetical studies on the various versions of the Life of Adam and Eve are:

G.A. Anderson, 'Celibacy or Consummation in the Garden? Reflections on Early Jewish and Christian Interpretations of the Garden of Eden', *HTR* 82 (1989), pp. 121-48.

—'The Penitence Narrative in the Life of Adam and Eve', *HUCA* 63 (1992), pp. 1-39.

D.A. Bertrand, *La vie grecque d'Adam et Eve* (Recherches intertestamentaires 1; Paris: Maisonneuve, 1987).

—'Le destin "post mortem" des protoplastes selon la "Vie grecque d'Adam et Eve"', in *La littérature intertestamentaire: Colloque de Strasbourg (17-19 octobre 1983)* (Paris: Presses Universitaires de France, 1985), pp. 109-18.

U. Bianchi, 'La rédemption dans les livres d'Adam', *Numen* 18 (1971), pp. 1-8.

A.B. Kolenkow, 'Trips to the Other World in Antiquity and the Story of Seth in the Life of Adam and Eve' (P.J. Achtemeier, ed.; SBLSP; Missoula: Scholars Press, 1977), pp. 1-11.

J.R. Levison, 'The Exoneration of Eve in the Apocalypse of Moses', *JSJ* 20 (1989), pp. 135-50.

—*Portraits of Adam in Early Judaism from Sirach to 2 Baruch* (JSPSup 1; Sheffield: JSOT Press, 1988).

G.W.E. Nickelsburg, 'Some Related Traditions in the Apocalypse of Adam, the Books of Adam and Eve and 1 Enoch', in B. Layton (ed.), *The Rediscovery of Gnosticism; vol. 2 Sethian Gnosticism* (Suppl. to *Numen* 41.2; Leiden: Brill, 1981), pp. 515-39.

E.C. Quinn, *The Quest of Seth for the Oil of Life* (Chicago: University of Chicago Press, 1962).

M.E. Stone, 'The Fall of Satan and Adam's Penance; Three notes on the Books of Adam and Eve', *JTS* NS 44 (1993), pp. 143-56.

A.M. Sweet, *A Religio-Historical Study of the Greek Life of Adam and Eve* (unpublished PhD dissertation; Notre Dame, 1992).

J. Tromp, 'Literary and Exegetical Issues in the Story of Adam's Death and Burial (GLAE 31-42)', in J. Frishman and L. van Rompay (eds.), *The Book of Genesis in Jewish and Oriental Christian Interpretation* (Traditio Exegetica Graeca, 5; Louvain: Peeters, 1997) (forthcoming).

E. Turdeanu, 'La *Vie d'Adam et d'Eve* en slave et en roumain', in *Apocryphes slaves et roumains de l'Ancien Testament* (SVTP, 5; Leiden: Brill, 1981), pp. 75-144 and pp. 437-38.

4

PROVENANCE AND DATE

Introduction

In the preceding chapters we have examined the *Life of Adam and Eve* as a specimen of ancient literature in continuous development. We have restricted ourselves to those texts that are recognizable stages in this development of a single literary work. In this chapter we come to the question of the origin of the *Life of Adam and Eve*, more particularly the origin of the text-form of *LAE* that the present authors regard as the earliest retraceable stage in the development of this writing, the 'short' *GLAE*: its date, place, language and milieu of origin.

There has been a time that these questions were thought to be the central and decisive issues in the interpretation of ancient writings. For several reasons, many scholars now regard these questions as subordinate or even irrelevant.

First of all, many modern scholars fail to see why the origin of a writing is important for its understanding at a later stage. It may be interesting to know, for instance, that the Slavonic *Life* derives (indirectly, perhaps) from a long Greek version, which in its turn depends on a shorter Greek version. Without that knowledge, however, the Slavonic *Life* can well be interpreted as such. Moreover, it has rightly become less natural to assume that an old, more primitive stage in a writing's development is intrinsically more important than later stages, especially if one acknowledges (as the present authors do) that later stages of the writing may contain traditions that are older than the earlier stages of the writing which do not contain those traditions.

There are also practical reasons to depreciate the question of origin. The history of the development of *LAE* through the centuries, as provisionally outlined in Chapter 2, exemplifies its nature of 'evolved literature'. If anywhere, it is shown in the *Life of Adam and Eve* that the 'most primitive' form of a writing can in no way be assumed to be the original. It must be accepted on principle that what the present authors take to be the source of all subsequent development (the 'short' *GLAE*) is itself just a stage (albeit an early stage) in the age-long process of the writing's evolution. One may wonder if, under such circumstances, it is at all worthwhile to attempt to speak about origins.

These insights are not new. Over half a century ago, the novelist Thomas Mann began his *Joseph and his Brethren* as follows:

> Tief ist der Brunnen der Vergangenheit. Sollte man ihn nicht unergründlich nennen?

Thomas Mann's doubts did not prevent him, however, from writing four books in over a thousand pages about Joseph and his family. Sometimes, he states, one must be content with the supposition of a specific primal starting point (*Ur-Beginn*) that is relevant for all practical purposes, even if one is well aware that one cannot seriously assume that in this way the bottomless pit of the past is fathomed.

We believe that the question of origin is relevant, because it helps to organize our own thoughts about the writing under discussion. We can all see the overwhelming abundance of legendary material about Adam and Eve, and how it has been recorded in numerous different writings. To use the image of a tree: if one wants to study it as a living organism, it is necessary to relate the unfolding of all its leaves and branches to the stem and roots to which they are attached, as well as to the soil conditions in which it rooted, and the climatological circumstances under which it grew.

So we ask in this chapter about the origin of the *Life* as a writing: where, when and why was it thought necessary to capture the traditions about Adam and Eve in a literary document? We do not ask these questions because we are more interested in the stem of the tree than in its leaves (more interested in timber, so to speak, than in the living organism), but because we are interested in the tree as a whole, and we believe that the study of its (assumed) beginning is a useful organizing principle in the reconstruction of its development.

Language and Place of Origin

In an excursus (written in co-operation with G. Bohak) of his *History* (see pp. 46-53), M.E. Stone has discussed the arguments that have been brought forward in favour of a Hebrew or Aramaic origin of the *Life of Adam and Eve*. After carefully examining a number of 'Hebraisms' in the Greek text, Bohak and Stone conclude that none of the evidence produced leads to the conclusion that *GLAE* was originally written in any other language than Greek. Stone remarks that 'this does not prove that the book was written in Greek' (p. 46), but this reservation seems overly cautious, because such proof is not called for. All versions available to us ultimately derive from a Greek text (Stone, *History*, p. 42); we do possess the writing in Greek, and there are no reasons to suppose that it is a translation from Hebrew or Aramaic. If it would appear that the Greek text is explicable only on account of certain translation errors, the hypothesis of another original language than Greek may prove useful. No such instances are known at present. Moreover, the Greek of *GLAE* may be bad Greek, measured by classical standards, but it is genuine Greek, containing, for instance, many syntactical constructions that are typical of that language.

We may conclude that it is safe to assume that *GLAE* was originally written in Greek.

It is hard to say anything meaningful about the geographical provenance of this writing. Its original language, Greek, provides no clue in this respect, since that language was spoken and written throughout the Hellenistic and Roman empires, not only in the Eastern Mediterranean (including Palestine), but in Rome and other Italian cities as well.

Ideological Provenance

The questions discussed in the previous section are closely connected with the question about the milieu in which *GLAE* originated: were its primary authors (non-Christian) Jews or Christians?

This question sheds light on the attempts made by earlier scholars to prove that *LAE* was first written in Hebrew. If that could be proven, it would be difficult to imagine that it was written anywhere else than in Palestine, and it would be practically certain that its origin was Jewish. The alleged Hebrew origin of the writing thus serves as unmistakable proof of its Palestinian-Jewish origin. Then, it is only a small step to reduce the question of its date of origin to that of before or after 70 CE We may not be too far off the mark when we suspect that the attempts to characterize *GLAE* as a *pre*-70, Palestinian-Jewish writing are connected with the presumption that there must be a relationship between *GLAE* and Paul's use of the Adam-traditions in Rom. 5.12-21 and 1 Cor. 15.21-22. It must be readily admitted that the Greek origin of *GLAE* does not preclude this provenance, but it is clear that the attempts to prove that the book is a translation are forced and prejudiced.

The question of Jewish or Christian provenance proves far more complicated. The problem is posed by the fact that all manuscripts of the *Life*, in whatever form or version, were produced by Christians. Moreover, most versions, including a good number of the Greek manuscripts, contain unmistakable references to Christ and the Christian creed. Only in the most primitive form of the text (the 'short' *GLAE*) is Christ not mentioned.

A relatively simple explanation for this state of affairs would be to assume that *GLAE* was originally a Jewish writing, adopted and edited by Christians. On the other hand, there are no fundamental objections against the view that *GLAE* contains traditional material which can easily be paralleled in Jewish literature, but that it is nevertheless an originally Christian document. Conceptually, the view that a book consisting of Jewish legends is originally Christian may seem complex. In terms of historical processes, however, the view that the writing was originally Christian and kept circulating in the Church is more readily acceptable than the view that a Jewish writing was adopted and edited by Christians. Again, the question of date is crucial, for the later the writing is thought to have been composed, the more difficult it is to imagine such a transition into the Church.

Several scholars have provided lists of specific details in the various versions of the *Life* which are paralleled in Jewish writings. A concise survey of these parallels can be found in Stone, *History*, pp. 58-60. However, as Stone rightly remarks, one needs to prove that such parallels 'can exist *only* in Jewish writings' (p. 58). One may go one step further and ask whether it is on principle possible to prove that Jewish material of this kind in any case excludes Christian usage. Even if a certain image or concept in *GLAE* could be paralleled only in Jewish writings, that still would be no proof of the Jewish origin of *GLAE*. The Christian world view permeates the members of the Church to such an extent that their eyes see everything in the light of Christ's pivotal role in world history. This all-encompassing world view is capable of absorbing practically any concept, image and word; the Christian editions of the Life are clear evidence of this fact, as is, for instance, the use of the Old Testament in the New Testament, and patristic exegesis of the Old Testament.

Earlier in this guide (p. 55), we asked whether a Christian *Life of Adam and Eve* is conceivable without mentioning Christ's salvific mediation. We believe that the answer must be that practically all Jewish (or, for that matter, non-Jewish, e.g., philosophical) traditions are conceivable in a Christian context, because Christians believe that everything is under the command of the God who revealed himself decisively in Jesus Christ, and are capable of understanding everything in the light of Christ, even if he is not mentioned. Therefore, it seems to us that adducing Jewish parallels to the *Life* can under no circumstance prove the Jewish origin of the *document*, but may just as well be taken as evidence of the incorporation of Jewish *traditions* in Christian circles (see H.F.D. Sparks, *The Apocryphal Old Testament*, p. 142).

The question of the Jewish or Christian origin of the *Life* cannot be decided by proving that it contains Jewish traditions that would be inconceivable in Christian writings. A more promising approach is to investigate whether the book contains Christian material unknown to Jewish tradition. If this is not the case, the question must remain undecided; if it is indeed the case, it must be established whether such a tradition may or may not be explained as a Christian interpolation. In other words: if we find distinctively Christian traditions that form an integrated part of the whole of the writing, we must seriously reckon with the possibility that the book was from the start written by Christians.

In the following paragraphs, we shall discuss three conspicuous elements in *GLAE* that at first sight give the impression that they might reflect a specific, possibly Christian background.

(a) When GLAE describes liturgical practices, *incense offerings* play an important role (e.g., 29.4; 33.4; 38.2). Since no offerings other than that of incense are mentioned, one is tempted to assume that these descriptions reflect the common usage of the Christian Church (it should be noted, however, that the offering of incense did not become usual in the Church until after the second half of the fourth century; see E. Fehrenbach, 'Encens', p. 6).

It is more likely, however, that the use of incense in Adam's and the heavenly liturgy reflects an ancient Jewish tradition, whereas the author of *GLAE* was not personally acquainted with this practice.

The tradition that Adam was the first to offer incense probably originated in priestly circles, as may be concluded from its presence in *Jub.* 3.27. In that passage it is said that the ingredients for the incense offering mentioned in Exod. 30.34 were taken by Adam from Paradise (a place well-known for its pleasant smell; cf. *1 En.* 29-32). Apparently, the author of *GLAE* 29.6 did know the tradition that Adam offered incense from Paradise, but was unaware of the recipe as given in Exodus. Assuming, of course, that Adam's offering would have to be pleasant, the author named four spices known for their agreeable scent (nard, saffron, calamus and cinnamon; cf. the list in Cant. 4.13-14, which includes these spices). It is unlikely, however, that the author was personally acquainted with the practice of incense offering, because the spices mentioned are not known to have served that purpose.

The offerings of incense can therefore not be taken as an indication of either Jewish or Christian origin of the *Life*. Whether the authors were Jewish or Christian, they probably did not know the ingredients for incense sacrifices, so that we may conclude that the description of these offerings do *not* reflect an actual liturgical practice.

(b) In *GLAE funerary rites* are described relatively elaborately. Apparently, great importance is attached to the proper way to bury people. If these rites contain specific elements, they might point to one provenance or the other.

From ch. 33 onwards the deaths and burials of Adam and Eve are related. First, it is described how the angels burn large amounts of frankincense near Adam (33.3-4); the angels and the sun and the moon pray for mercy on the deceased one (33.5–36.2). After an angel has announced God's decision in favour of Adam (37.1-2), a Seraph washes him three times in the Acherusian lake and makes him lay down for three hours (37.3-4). Then, God hands Adam over to Michael, and commands that he be brought to Paradise in the third heaven (37.4-5); all the angels praise God for his mercy (37.6). It seems that the description of Adam being washed and laid out for three hours does not immediately reflect actual funerary practices, because the Acherusian lake is conceived as a real lake, wherever it may be, and unattainable for living people (see below). Of course, rites may have been performed to symbolize this event, but it is more likely that the description in chs. 33–37 of Adam's *post mortem* existence cannot be connected with the rites surrounding actual burial of the dead, since that seems to be the subject of the following sequence.

Again, angels descend to the body of Adam, holding frankincense-burners in their hands (38.2-3). They go into Paradise which also gives off strong fragrances, which make everybody fall asleep, except Seth, who witnesses the following events (38.4). God bewails Adam and promises the resurrection (39.1-3). He tells Michael to fetch three shrouds of linen and silk from Paradise in the third heaven, and the archangels cover Adam in these shrouds and pour sweet-smelling oils upon him (40.1-2). After the body of Abel has been treated in the same way (40.3-5), they bring both bodies to a place near Paradise, to the place where God had taken the earth from which he had formed Adam; there, the angels dig a grave for both bodies (40.6). Adam and Abel are buried with many perfumes from Paradise (40.7). At the grave, God announces to Adam that he is dust and will return to dust, but that God will eventually raise him and his offspring (41.1-3). To conclude the ceremony, God seals the monument on Adam's grave with a triangular seal, which is to remain there for six days, until his wife will join him in his grave (42.1).

If we strip from this story the elements that are proper to the special events related, the rites that this description may reflect are the following: (a) burning of frankincense; (b) bewailing of the deceased; (c) covering of the body in shrouds and embalming it with sweet-smelling oil; (d) placing the body in a grave dug for the purpose; (e) a speech at the grave, in contemplation of human mortality and the promised resurrection; (f) sealing the monument on the grave with a triangular seal.

It should be stressed that it is not at all sure that these elements really reflect actual rites used in the days of the authors of *GLAE*. Only when Eve has been buried as well, the archangel Michael instructs Seth to bury every man or woman who has died 'in this way' (43.2). But in Eve's case, no rites are described, so that it remains unclear what way is meant. It may be that this passage intends to say no more than that people must be buried (as opposed to, for instance, being left unburied or being burnt), or that one should dress a dead body before burying (the word which corresponds with 'to dress' in the Armenian and Georgian translations is in this instance equivocal in Greek: it may refer to the laying out of a body or to its burial proper).

In any case, there seem to be few characteristic elements in Adam's burial that might point to the provenance of the writing. Shrouds as well as sweet-smelling oil and other fragrances make a perfectly natural impression and can be expected anywhere in antiquity; therefore, the parallel usually quoted in this connection, Jn 19.39-40 (cf. Mk 16.1), does not necessarily indicate a Christian origin of *GLAE* (cf. the phrase in Jn 19.40 'according to the Jewish custom').

One element, however, is intriguing: Adam's grave is sealed off with a triangular seal. As far as we know, this practice is unparalleled. In Matt. 27.66, it is told that Pilate had Jesus' grave sealed up, but there this action has a clear function: the author gives this detail to prove that

Jesus' body was not stolen by his followers, but was indeed raised from the dead by God (cf. Matt. 27.62–28.6). In *GLAE*, however, no such function is evident. One could guess that the seal was perhaps thought to avert evil powers that might disturb the sleep of the dead. However, according to *GLAE* 42.1, the seal was to remain on Adam's grave for six days only, until Eve's body would be joined to his.

A further question is raised by the fact that the seal is said to be triangular. In her *A Religio-Historical Study of the Greek Life of Adam and Eve* (PhD Dissertation; Notre Dame, 1992) Anne Marie Sweet remarks that *GLAE* has a certain predilection for the number three, whereas the triangle was associated in the Hellenistic world with perfection and immortality (pp. 194-95). On the other hand, it cannot be denied that in the early Church, too, the number three was immensely important, also in connection with the baptism. What is more, the early Church considered the baptism as a 'seal': those who were baptized ('sealed') were owned by Christ. Baptism itself was often accompanied by a gesture signifying the cross and performed in the name of the Trinity (see Lampe, *A Patristic Greek Lexicon*, 1253b-1254b s. v. *stauros*, and 1355a-1357a s. v. *sphragis*). It is true that the designation of the baptism as a seal is not qualified by its triangularity elsewhere. But it is also true that Christian baptism and the number three are intimately associated. In this connection, it is worthwhile mentioning that according to *GLAE* 37.3 Adam was washed three times in the Acherusian lake before he entered Paradise in the third heaven; likewise, baptism could be performed by three immersions in water (Lampe, *A Patristic Greek Lexicon*, 285a s. v. *baptisma*; see further below, on the Acherusian lake).

It seems that the description of Adam's burial may well be understood in the light of the description of Jesus' burial in the Gospels: their bodies are shrouded and embalmed with fragrances, and their tombs are sealed off. The seal on Adam's grave was associated with baptism, and thus with the number three. The triangular seal, because of its seemingly total lack of function in the context, is the main reason for our assumption that the details in the description of Adam's burial were provided by Christian authors. One should reckon with the possibility, however, that the element that Adam's grave was sealed was inserted in a later stage, namely when a Christian scribe associated the tending of Adam's body with that for Jesus' body according to the Gospels, and therefore added the detail of the sealing of the grave. The shrouds and the fragrances do not by themselves indicate a Christian origin.

(c) In *GLAE* 37.3 we read that one of the six-winged seraphs carries Adam off to the *Acherusian lake* and washes him three times before conducting him before God's throne. This happens after the angels, supported by sun and moon, have entreated God to show mercy to Adam and, later, have praised him for being merciful. 'Blessed be the glory of the Lord over his works; he has had mercy on Adam, the work of his hands' (33.1–37.2). After Adam has lain in front of God's throne for three hours, God hands him over to Michael to take him to Paradise in the third heaven (37.4-6).

The nearest parallels to this are found in some early Christian texts. The river and/or the lake Acheron are traditionally the place where the souls of those who have sinned in their lives are purified (see e. g. Plato, *Phaedo* 113 a, d). There are no Jewish texts where the Acherusian lake is mentioned—as is admitted by E. Peterson, who in his informative article 'Die "Taufe" im Acherusischen See' (1955) has tried hard to find Jewish antecedents to this Christian apocalyptic tradition. The principal parallels are the following:

The Greek 'Rainer-fragment' parallel to *Apocalypse of Peter* 14 (in the Ethiopic version) reads: 'Then I will give to my called and my chosen whomsoever they shall ask me for, out of torment, and will give them a fair baptism to salvation from the Acherusian lake which men so call in the Elysian Field, even a portion of righteousness with my holy ones' (trans. J.K. Elliott; *ANT*, p. 609 n. 1). One notes that the righteous intercede for sinners who are allowed to join the elect after being cleansed in the Acherusian lake. The same is found in the Christian(-ized) passage *Sib. Or.* 2.330-339, where those for whom the pious make intercession are sent by God 'to another eternal life with the immortals in the Elysian plain where he has the long waves of the deep perennial Acherusian lake' (trans. J.J. Collins in J.H. Charlesworth, *OTP* I, p. 353).

Some later, and less close parallels may be mentioned. In the *Apocalypse of Paul* 22 the Acherusian lake presents a new chance to the sinner who is converted and repents and bears fruits worthy of repentance. 'When he has gone out of the body he is brought and worships God, and thence by command of the Lord he is delivered to the angel Michael, and he baptizes him in the Acherusian lake—then he leads him into the City of Christ alongside those who have never sinned' (trans. Elliott, *ANT*, 629-630). In the *Book of the Resurrection of Jesus Christ by Bartholomew the Apostle* 21.6 Michael plunges the soul after death three times in the lake Acheron (see J.D. Kaestli and P. Cherix, *L'évangile de Barthélémy* [1993], p. 230).

On the basis of the comparison of *GLAE* 37.3 with the passages just mentioned we may conclude that at least the section of *GLAE* 31–37, of which this verse forms an essential element, received its present form from a Christian redactor–author. The *Apocalypse of Peter* is quoted by Clement of Alexandria and generally dated in the first half of the second century CE.

Surveying these specific elements, it must be concluded that the case for either the Jewish or the Christian origin of *LAE* is weak. A decision hinges mainly on the question whether the mention of the Acherusian lake is a sufficient indication for the Christian origin of the book as a whole. There is no reason to assume that the mention of the lake was interpolated, and *GLAE* 31–37 are an essential section of the writing. Given the continuity of Jewish traditions in the Christian Church (which can account for the distinctly Jewish 'flavour' of *GLAE*), and because of the more simple historical process such a hypothesis presupposes, the present authors have a clear preference for the assumption that *GLAE* was first composed by Christian authors.

The Christian origin of *GLAE*, if it is accepted, may also help to answer the question why this document was written. In the early Christian literature a certain interest in the figure of Adam is apparent. The antithesis between Adam and Christ was an important issue in the Church since the apostle Paul used it (Paul may not have been the first to introduce the antithesis, but his writings obviously furthered its usage). It may even be that because Christians put Adam on the theological agenda, he became a topic in Jewish writings, such as *2 Baruch* and *4 Ezra*, as well. Naturally, we do not wish to suggest that *2 Baruch* and *4 Ezra* are dependent on the epistles of Paul. It cannot be excluded, however, that the importance of Adam in the Christian world attracted the theological attention of non-Christian Jews.

Be that as it may, the interest of Christians for Adam as the anti-type of Christ is evident, and it is readily conceivable that Christians, spurred by this interest, found it worthwhile to record the story of Adam's fall, his condemnation, death and the resurrection promised to him. To compose this story, they used traditional material available to them, much of which was already of Jewish origin, but had never been written down before. The *Life of Adam and Eve* may then be seen as a document originally written by its authors to set out in detail what role the protoplasts had played in the history of mankind.

It should be noted, however, that the authors of *GLAE* did not make the antithesis of Adam and Christ the starting-point of their exposition. For them, that initially theological concern took the form of a more general interest in the figure of Adam. They apparently took the traditional stories about Adam as their lead, and felt no urge to bend them towards their Christian faith.

Later editions of the *Life* did include references to Christ, inserted more or less automatically by editors who were guided by the Christian creed. It is made explicit in these later editions that Adam received grace for the sake of Christ, even though the latter was still to perform his salvific task. Even then, all traces of the antithesis that had awakened interest in this figure in the first place are missing, and the view of Adam is identical to that in the earliest stage of the writing, the 'short' *GLAE*.

So the story of Adam and Eve simply came to be adopted into the early Christian mythology without any specifically Christian adjustments, except that it is told as the story of humanity that needs redemption.

Date

The date of *GLAE* is the most difficult historical question to solve. The obvious way of settling this question is by investigating when the writing was quoted for the first time. A large number of references in early Christian literature to Adam-books can be found in Stone's *History*, pp. 75-83. We shall briefly glance at some of these.

In the first place, there are lists of apocrypha in which Adam-books feature. If the *Poenitentia Adae* mentioned in the Decree of Ps.-Gelasius is the same as our writing, it pre-dates the sixth century (when the Gelasian Decree was composed; text in E. von Dobschütz, *Das Decretum Gelasianum* [1912], pp. 346-52). In the *Apostolic Constitutions* VI 16, 1 (to be dated around 380; there is no corresponding passage in the *Didascalia*, a main source of the *Constitutions*) it is said that some apocryphal books of Moses, Enoch, Adam, and others are known, but may not be accepted as canonical (ed. M. Metzger, *Les constitutions apostoliques* II [1986], pp. 344-46). In other lists of apocryphal books, such as the *Stichometry* of Nicephorus (ninth century; text in Th. Zahn, *Geschichte des neutestamentlichen Kanons* II, 1 [1890], pp. 295-301), Adam-books feature as well.

George Syncellus († 810) claims to have seen a book called *The Life of Adam*, and speaks of its contents (the writing was known to Anastasius Sinaita [seventh century] as the *Testament of the Protoplasts*;

see W. Adler, *Time Immemorial* [1989], p. 103). According to Syncellus, this *Life of Adam* contained the numbers of the respective days on which Adam named the animals, entered Paradise, transgressed the commandments, and so forth (ed. A.A. Mosshammer, *Georgius Syncellus* [1984], pp. 4-5).

This account of the *Life of Adam* evidently does not correspond to our *GLAE* (see H. Gelzer, *Sextus Julius Africanus* II [1885], p. 266). Later on, Syncellus relates that Seth was taken up to heaven and received revelations about the future, about Adam's impending fall, about the flood, and about the advent of the Saviour; also, Seth is supposed to have told his parents what had been revealed to him by the angels (Mosshammer, p. 9). *GLAE* 3.2 seems to allude to a tradition of this kind. In this passage, it is said that Seth will reveal to Adam everything the latter will do. However, *GLAE* pays no further attention to this matter. Moreover, Syncellus does not ascribe this information to his *Life of Adam*.

It must be concluded, therefore, that it is by no means certain that the titles mentioned in the lists of apocrypha actually refer to our *LAE*. There are many writings with titles containing the name 'Adam', and they are not at all identical (see below, Chapter 5). Therefore, a title alone is no sure indication of what writing is intended, and the lists of apocryphal books do not help in dating *GLAE*.

Another way of dating our writing would be to see when it was used in another writing for the first time. But in this case, one should be extremely cautious. The traditions concerning the life of Adam and Eve were numerous and widespread. It is often unnecessary to assume that documents containing passages that parallel elements in the account of *LAE* actually quote from that writing (see again below, Chapter 5).

A positive date *ante quem* can only be furnished by a quotation that is marked as such, or by a passage that is otherwise likely to depend on *LAE*. No instances of the former category are known to the present authors; as set out above (in Chapter 2, pp. 38-39), the *Descensus ad inferos* (at one moment incorporated in the *Gospel of Nicodemus*) is most likely to be an example of the latter. However, the character of this *Gospel* and the *Descensus* as 'evolved literature' is not much different from that of *LAE*, that is, it is as difficult to date the *Gospel of Nicodemus* and its various stages as it is to date the *Life*. A relative date is all we can attain: the *Gospel* (including the *Descensus*) is younger than the *Life*. To conclude more from this would be explaining the *obscurum per obscurius*.

Since there is no 'hard' evidence by which to date *GLAE*, we need to resort to educated guesses. The following observations should be taken into consideration.

(a) The Latin manuscript BN latin 5327 is a copy from an original dating between 730 and 740 CE (see Stone, *History*, p. 18). The text of this manuscript, belonging to Meyer's group IV, represents a developed stage of the Latin version (see Chapter 1, pp. 14-15), which itself is of a very secondary nature as compared to the Greek text (see Chapter 2, pp. 37-40). The Latin version of the *Life* represents the latest stage in the writing's development; before this version was made, other versions and editions had spread already all over the Eastern Christian world.

(b) There are parallels (as well as important differences) between *GLAE* on the one hand and such writings as the *Discourse on Abbatôn* (fourth to sixth centuries), the *Cave of Treasures* (third to sixth centuries), and the *Apocalypse of Adam* (second to third centuries) on the other; for a discussion of these writings (and their uncertain dates, which are, moreover, often established with reference to *GLAE*), see below, Chapter 5. Although it is not possible to establish direct literary links between *GLAE* and the documents cited, it would seem unwise to date *GLAE* later than these works.

(c) The assumption of the Christian origin of *GLAE* would seem to preclude a date earlier than 100 CE.

In view of these considerations, it would seem possible to date *GLAE* to anywhere between 100 and 600 CE. In the light of the extensive development of the writing and the interlacement with other writings through its traditional material, it would seem safe to posit its origin not too late in this period, i.e., in the second to fourth centuries.

A final remark: In her *A Religio-Historical Study of the Greek Life of Adam and Eve* Anne Marie Sweet has strongly underlined the non-apocalyptic and non-gnostic character of the Greek *Life of Adam and Eve*. She even goes a significant step further in positing that its authors were aware of apocalyptic and gnostic interpretations of the Genesis stories concerning Adam and Eve and intentionally defended more traditional views. 'It is our contention that the *Bios* (i.e. *GLAE*) has taken those elements of the Genesis story which have been "distorted" in Gnostic tradition and incorporated them into a reworking of the Genesis story in such a way so as to reaffirm a "conventional" reading of the biblical text' (p. 90). Sweet rightly emphasizes the great difference between *GLAE* and gnostic texts; in our view she has, however, not been able to prove her thesis that *GLAE* knew gnostic (and other) portraits of Adam and Eve and wanted to correct them.

Editions and Translations

Those used in this chapter are the following.

E. von Dobschütz, *Das Decretum Gelasianum de libris recipiendis et non recipiendis* (Texte und Untersuchungen 38, 4; Leipzig: Hinrichs, 1912).

J.K. Elliott, *The Apocryphal New Testament* (Oxford: Clarendon Press, 1993).

J.D. Kaestli and P. Cherix, *L'évangile de Barthélémy d'après deux écrits apocryphes* (Turnhout: Brepols, 1993).

M. Metzger (ed.), *Les constitutions apostoliques* II (Sources chrétiennes 329; Paris: Cerf, 1986).

A.A. Mosshammer (ed.), *Georgius Syncellus: Ecloga chronographica* (Leipzig: Teubner, 1984).

F. Scheidweiler, 'Nikodemusevangelium, Pilatusakten und Höllenfahrt Christi' in W. Schneemelcher, *Neutestamentliche Apokryphen* I (Tübingen: Mohr, 5th edn, 1989), pp. 395-424.

C. Tischendorf, ''Υπομνήματα τοῦ κυρίου ἡμῶν Ἰησοῦ Χριστοῦ πραχθέντα ἐπὶ Πόντιου Πιλάτου; Gesta Pilati; Evangelii Nicodemi pars altera sive Descensus Christi ad inferos', in *Evangelia apocrypha* (Leipzig, 2nd edn, 1876; repr. Hildesheim: Olms, 1966), pp. 210-432.

Th. Zahn, *Geschichte des neutestamentlichen Kanons* II, 1 (Erlangen–Leipzig: Deichert, 1890).

Further Reading

W. Adler, *Time Immemorial: Archaic History and its Sources in Christian Chronography from Julius Africanus to George Syncellus* (Dumbarton Oaks Studies 26; Washington: Dumbarton Oaks, 1989).

E. Fehrenbach, 'Encens' in: *Dictionnaire d'archéologie chrétienne et de liturgie* V, 1 (Paris: Letouzey, 1922), cols. 2-21.

H. Gelzer, *Sextus Julius Africanus und die byzantinische Chronologie* II (Leipzig, 1885).

G.W.H. Lampe, *A Patristic Greek Lexicon* (Oxford: Clarendon Press, 1961).

E. Peterson, 'Die "Taufe" im Acherusischen See', *Vigiliae Christianae* 9 (1955), pp. 1-20 = idem, *Frühkirche, Judentum und Gnosis* (Rome–Freiburg–Vienna: Herder, 1959), pp. 310-32.

A.M. Sweet, *A Religio-Historical Study of the Greek Life of Adam and Eve* (unpublished PhD Dissertation; Notre Dame, 1992).

5

SECONDARY ADAM LITERATURE

Introductory Matters

In the past many authors of introductions to the Greek and Latin versions of the *Life of Adam and Eve* have referred to other books on Adam and Eve more or less related to these. Among them may be mentioned J.-B. Frey with his article 'Adam (Livres apocryphes sous son nom)' (1928), pp. 101-134 and A.-M. Denis who, in Chapter 1 of his *Introduction aux pseudépigraphes grecs d'Ancien Testament* (1970) not only discusses the *Life of Adam and Eve* but also devotes attention to 'Le cycle d'Adam' (pp. 7-14). In the second revised and expanded edition of that book (which is in course of preparation) considerably more information about these later, Christian and Gnostic, books will be given.

The best introduction to this so-called secondary Adam literature can be found in M.E. Stone's *A History of the Literature of Adam and Eve*, a book repeatedly referred to above. There the author gives in chapter 3 (pp. 75-83) a list of 'Testimonia and References to Adam Books', followed in chapter 4 (pp. 84-123) by a survey of 'Secondary Adam Literature'. Stone mentions Adam writings in Greek, Latin, Syriac, Ethiopic, Arabic, Armenian, Georgian, Coptic, Old Irish, Slavonic and Hebrew; he also deals with other mediaeval Adam writings and has an appendix on Gnostic and Mandean Adam texts. In his introduction to Chapter 4 the author warns us that his list is far from complete and that he will concentrate on the early books belonging to this category and on those which are directly or indirectly influenced by the primary Adam books. Nevertheless his treatment of the literature involved is extremely useful as a starting point for further detailed study. In particular his section on Armenian Adam books, where he has done a lot of pioneering work himself, will be welcomed.

There is little point in repeating the work of Stone in the present guide. After due consideration we have selected the following among the many writings that could be dealt with: the *Discourse on Abbatôn* already mentioned in connection with the Coptic fragments (see p. 17), the *Testament of Adam*, the *Cave of Treasures*, the *Conflict of Adam and Eve with Satan and the Apocalypse of Adam*. They have been chosen because of (possible) connections between traditional elements found in them with those in one or more versions of the *Life of Adam and Eve*.

In establishing the relationships between the different versions of the *Life of Adam and Eve* several methods were applied: textual and literary criticism and also tradition criticism (see e.g. pp. 28-30). When, however, we ask to what extent the *Life of Adam and Eve*, in one of its forms, was known to and used by the authors of the secondary Adam books, we can only establish relations between *traditions* with any degree of certainty. This point has to be stressed, both in regard to the study of the secondary Adam books and in regard to a right assessment of the writings discussed in the first chapters of this guide. The latter, as we have seen, present various stages in the development of Adam traditions, individually and (particularly) combined to form more or less coherent stories. Not surprisingly certain traditional elements crop up elsewhere, also in the secondary Adam literature, in other contexts and often also in a different form serving another purpose. It is meaningful to analyse the agreements and the differences, but that is something different from trying to establish direct or indirect influence from the different versions of the *Life of Adam and Eve* as documents—especially from the Greek *Life* in the earliest form that can be established with text-critical methods. In order to draw conclusions concerning a literary-critical relationship of some sort we would have to establish dependence on one, or preferably more, constitutive elements in one of the versions of the *Life*, and that seems to be impossible.

Further Reading

A.-M. Denis, *Introduction aux pseudépigraphes grecs d'Ancien Testament* (SVTP 1; Leiden: Brill, 1970), pp. 3-14.

J.-B. Frey, 'Adam (Livres apocryphes sous son nom)' in *Dictionnaire de la Bible. Supplément* (Paris: Letouzey et Ané, 1928), I, pp. 101-34.

The *Discourse on Abbatôn*

The *Discourse on Abbatôn, the Angel of Death* is a homily ascribed to Timothy, Archbishop of Alexandria around 380. It has come down to us in a Coptic (Sahidic) manuscript (dated in 982 ce), and its text was edited and translated by E.A.W. Budge (see p. 17). It is not certain that it is a genuine work of Timothy. C.D.G. Müller (*Die Engellehre der Koptischen Kirche* [1959], pp. 273-75) dates it anywhere from the fourth to the sixth century. The homily purports to give the contents of a book about the appointment of Abbatôn (= Abaddon, cf. Rev. 9.11) as angel of death, containing information given by Jesus to Peter, after his resurrection. We shall briefly survey the account insofar as it is of interest to us.

When God the Father wishes to create Adam from virgin earth, according to his image and likeness, the earth protests vehemently. After many failed missions by other angels, only the angel Mouriêl has the courage to bring to God what he has asked for. Adam is fashioned and after 40 days the breath of life is breathed into his nostrils. Father and Son foresee what will happen later. God warns his Son that he will be obliged to go down to earth and to suffer on Adam's behalf, in order to redeem him and to bring him back to his primal state. The Son agrees to be his advocate.

Adam worships God and is set on a great throne with a crown of glory. All angels have to worship him, but one of them refuses, with his followers. His name is not mentioned but he is clearly very powerful; only with great difficulty is he defeated and cast down upon the earth, where his followers become devils with him. His argument for not worshipping is: 'It is meet that this [man Adam] should come and worship me, for I existed before he came into being' (trans. Budge, p. 483).

Eve is made from Adam's rib and in the form of Adam. They live in Paradise for two hundred years, as virgins ('and they were even as the angels of God' [Budge, p. 484]). Then Eve, tending the animals in the northern part of Paradise, is seduced by the devil. Day and night the devil has lain in wait for Adam and Eve near Paradise, and finally he takes his chance when he sees Eve alone. He speaks through the mouth of the serpent when he comes 'at the hour of evening to receive his food according to his wont'. Eve gives in to the temptation of the devil and Adam, after much protesting, gives in to Eve, who declares that she will take the blame.

The serpent, Eve and Adam are punished by God. To Adam God predicts a difficult life of 930 years, and 4500 years in the underworld. After 5500 years are fulfilled the Son will come on earth. During the thirty-five and a half years of his life he will perform many miracles, but nevertheless he will have to suffer and to die on the cross. He will go down to the underworld and deliver Adam. God says: 'He shall bring thee up therefrom together with all those who shall be held there in captivity with thee. For thy sake, O Adam, the Son of God shall suffer all these things until He hath redeemed thee, and restored thee to Paradise, unto the place whence thou didst come' (Budge, p. 488).

Next, the expulsion from Paradise and a conversation between the devil and Adam outside the Garden (in which Satan promises perpetual enmity because Adam was the cause of his being deprived from the heavenly glory) are reported. Mouriêl is appointed by God as Angel of Death, very harsh and cruel, and horrible to look at. 'Thus thou shalt continue to be king over them until the period for which I have ordained the world [to last] shall be ended' (Budge, p. 490). Even the angels are terrified when they see Abbatôn and lament the fate of the human beings to be born into the world. Abbatôn, however, asks and receives permission to deal kindly with those who are afraid of him, give alms and charities in his name, and commemorate the thirteenth days of the month Hathor, the day of Abbatôn's appointment. Their names will be written in the Book of Life, and they will take part in God's Kingdom.

The story of the creation of Adam and Eve, and of their disobedience and its consequences for humanity, are here part of the larger story of human sin and the salvation by Jesus Christ—with special emphasis on the relation between humanity and the Angel of Death, the central figure in this homily. Readers familiar with the different versions of the *Life of Adam and Eve* immediately recognize a number of points of contact between those writings and this homily:

There is, of course, the story of Satan's pride, protest and fall (see chs. 11–17 in Arm.–Georg. and Lat.), in *LAE* told by Satan in a meeting with Adam and Eve after their expulsion from Paradise. The argument of seniority mentioned here is found also in 16.2-3 (Gr., Arm.–Georg.). Next there is the co-operation between serpent and devil, found here and in chs. 16–19 (Gr., Arm.–Georg.) with the details of the serpent, like all other animals, dependent on the distribution of food by Adam and Eve (16.3 in Gr., clearer in 16.2-3 in Arm.–Georg.) and of Eve taking the blame (see *LAE* 21.4 in Georg., where Arm. is missing). Also in 7.2 (Gr., Arm.–Georg., Lat.) and 17.1-2 (Gr., Arm.–Georg.) the devil waits until Eve is alone. Finally there is a connection between the story here of the restitution of Adam by Jesus Christ after 5500 years (in itself a traditional figure) and the latter's descent into the underworld, and the short references to these events found in the

Arm.–Georg. and Lat. equivalent of *GLAE* 13.3-5.

These parallels are interesting, but they are insufficient to prove that the author of the homily knew the *Life of Adam and Eve*, and even less that he knew the *Life* in a (Greek or Coptic) version similar to the one we know to underlie the Armenian and Georgian. The author was familiar with a number of traditions also found in various versions of the *Life*, and it is helpful to note that those were known in Egypt. Whether they were taken from a *Life of Adam and Eve*, or even of the Coptic document of which we posses some fragments, we simply do not know.

Further Reading

E.A.W. Budge, 'The Discourse on Abbatôn', in his *Coptic Martyrdoms etc. in the Dialect of Upper Egypt* (London: British Museum, 1914), pp. x-xi; xxii-xxiii; lxviii-lxxii (introductions and summary), pp. 225-49 (text) and pp. 482-91 (translation).

C.D.G. Müller, *Die Engellehre der Koptischen Kirche* (Wiesbaden: Harrassowitz, 1959).

The *Testament of Adam*

The most recent edition of the *Testament of Adam* is that of S.E. Robinson in his *The Testament of Adam* (1982; see also his contribution to J.H. Charlesworth, *OTP* I [1983], pp. 989-95). The Syriac *Testament of Adam* which he edited is found in three recensions, witnessed by eight manuscripts dating between the early ninth and late eighteenth centuries. It is divided into three sections: a Horarium (the hours of the day and of the night), a Prophecy in the form of a testament from Adam to Seth, and the 'Hierarchy' (a list of the nine orders of heavenly beings and a description of their functions). The Hierarchy is found in only one Syriac manuscript (written in 1702). There are versions of (parts of) this *Testament* in Greek, Arabic, Ethiopic, Armenian and Georgian, but Robinson considers these all (even the Greek) as secondary. See also Stone, *History*, pp. 95-97 and *idem*, *Armenian Apocrypha relating to the Patriarchs and Prophets* (1982), pp. 39-51.

The provenance of the three sections is a matter of dispute, as are the coherence of the book and the date of its (Christian) redaction. Robinson thinks that the book dates from the middle or late third century CE, but his evidence is, as so often in dating similar writings, circumstantial. For our present purpose the most interesting section is the Prophecy. It is definitely Christian, but it shows acquaintance with Adam traditions found in Jewish sources and, according to some, also with the *Life of Adam and Eve*.

We hear how Adam tells his son Seth that God will come into the world as a human being born from a virgin. God told him so himself when Adam 'picked some of the fruit in which death was hiding' (3.2). Surprisingly God's words were: 'Adam, Adam, do not fear. You wanted to be a god. I will make you a god, not right now but after a space of many years.' Because Adam listened to the words of the serpent, he and his posterity will be food for the serpent. But, as he is created in God's image, God–Christ promises him: 'I will set you at the right hand of my divinity, and I will make you a god just like you wanted' (3.4).

Next Adam predicts the Flood because of the daughters of Cain 'who killed your brother Abel because of passion for your sister Lebuda, since sins have been created through your mother Eve'. The end of the world will be 6000 years after the Flood (3.5).

Seth, as the author of Adam's testament, tells how Adam was borne to his grave (at the East of Paradise, opposite the city of Enoch) because he had been created in the image of God. The sun and the moon were darkened for seven days. The testament was sealed and put into the Cave of Treasures (see next section) 'with the offerings Adam had taken out of Paradise, gold and myrrh and frankincense' (3.7)—later to be brought by the magi to the cave in Bethlehem where the Son of God was born.

This survey has followed the text of recension 1 (in Robinson's translation). Recension 2, which generally gives a shorter text, adds the interesting detail that the fruit eaten by Adam was a fig.

As to the parallels with the *Life of Adam and Eve* we note that the description of the consequences of Adam's sin and his restitution to former splendour again recalls the Arm.–Georg. and Lat. equivalent of *GLAE* 13.3-5. Next there is Adam's burial by angels and the darkening of the sun and moon, also found in *LAE* chs. 38–42 and chs. 34–36 respectively (in Gr., Arm.–Georg. and Lat.). As to the offerings which Adam had taken out of Paradise: they remind us of ch. 29.3-6 in Gr. and Arm.–Georg., but the gold, myrrh and frankincense are clearly taken from Matt. 2.11.

For the mention of the fig as the forbidden fruit reference is sometimes made to *GLAE* 20.5. This notice is, however, a secondary as well as corrupt reading in manuscripts ATLCRM, caused by iotacism (Nagel, *La vie grecque* I, pp. 72-73). The idea that the fig was the forbidden fruit is found, however, in *Gen. R.* 15.7. Sisters of Cain and Abel are mentioned several times in rabbinic sources (see L. Ginzberg, *The*

Legends of the Jews [1909–38], I, pp. 108-109 and V, pp. 138-39).

These parallels show that the Christian *Testament of Adam* had access to earlier traditions about Adam. There is no proof for an earlier Jewish form of the Prophecy, nor for literary dependence of the *Testament* on any form of the *Life of Adam and Eve*.

Further Reading

S.E. Robinson, *The Testament of Adam* (SBLDS 52; Chico, CA: Scholars Press, 1982).

—'Testament of Adam' in J. H. Charlesworth, *The Old Testament Pseudepigrapha* (Garden City, NY: Doubleday, 1983), I, pp. 989-95.

L. Ginzberg, *The Legends of the Jews*, 7 vols. (Philadelphia: Jewish Publication Society, 1909–38).

The *Cave of Treasures*

The *Cave of Treasures* is a history of biblical events down to the coming of Christ, which has had an extensive influence on Oriental Christian literature (see Stone, *History*, pp. 90-95). It was written in Syriac, and there are translations in Arabic and Ethiopic (as parts of larger works), in Georgian and in Coptic (only fragmentary). The most recent edition of the Syriac (with French translation) is that by Su-Min Ri, *La Caverne des Trésors* (1987). He was able to use 19 manuscripts, divided into an Eastern and a Western family. An English translation is given in E.A.W. Budge, *The Book of the Cave of Treasures* (1927).

The *Cave of Treasures* is commonly thought to date from the sixth century, but is is assumed that it used an earlier document existing already in the fourth, with earlier sources. Su-Min Ri (*Translation*, pp. xxii-xxiii) puts the redaction of the writing in the third century.

What is said about Adam and Eve in this book may be summarized as follows. After Adam is formed in God's image and likeness, he is dressed in royal robes and wears a glorious crown; dominion over the entire creation is given to him by God (2.17-24). Satan becomes jealous and refuses to prostrate himself before Adam (3.1-2). He is then expelled from heaven, whereas Adam is taken up to Paradise, where the angels praise him (3.4-8). There Eve is made from Adam's rib and together they are dressed in glory (3.11-14). When the devil sees this, again jealousy takes hold of him (4.4). He takes up his dwelling inside the serpent, goes to Paradise (4.5) and watches Eve until she is alone (4.12), and then seduces her into eating the forbidden fruit. Immediately she finds herself naked and Adam, too, after having eaten is nude (4.15, 18).

Adam is, however, not punished according to the *Cave of Treasures*. The earth is damned on account of Adam's sins and the serpent as well as Eve are punished, but Adam himself receives no punishment (5.4-5). His fate will be to live on the damned earth until the time of the coming of God's son on earth, born from a virgin (5.7-8). In 48.7-8 we hear that this will take place after 5500 years. God also tells Adam to instruct his sons about the embalming of his body after his death, and its burial in the 'Cave of Treasures'. There he will stay until he will be brought to the blessed land (5.10 in the Western manuscripts, variant: 'the outside world', in the Eastern ones).

Having left Paradise Adam and Eve find a cave nearby on the mountain which they consecrate as a prayer-house for themselves. They call it the 'Cave of Treasures' (5.17). They had remained virgins until that time, but now Adam and Eve have intercourse; and as a result Abel and his twin sister Climna (or Climtha), as well as Cain and his twin sister Labuda are born (5.18-20). The row between Cain and Abel starts with a dispute over who is to take which sister as his wife (5.21-23).

After a century of mourning for Abel, Seth is born; he is described as a handsome giant. When Adam is dying, at the age of 930, he calls his sons, including Seth, and delivers his farewell speech (6.1-14). His most remarkable instruction is his commandment to Seth and his progeny to take his body from the Cave of Treasures when they leave the regions of Paradise, and to bring it to the centre of the earth (6.12). Adam is embalmed by Seth and is buried in the Cave of Treasures after a mourning period of 140 days (6.15-21).

Seth guides his people in righteousness and takes them to the mountain around the Cave, keeping them separate from Cain and his offspring who live further down in the plain. The Sethites live in purity, holiness, peace and happiness until Seth, in turn, is also buried in the Cave (ch. 7). The children of Seth stick to his rules until the days of Jared, when they go down from the holy mountain and mingle with Cainite women (Gen. 6.1-4!) (ch. 10). In the end only Noah, Shem, Ham and Japheth and their wives keep apart, and they are the ones saved in the Flood (chs. 16–20). At Lamech's command Noah takes the body of Adam with him in the ark (while his sons carry the three offerings of gold, myrrh and frankincense), and later Shem indeed brings Adam's body to the place where it belongs: Golgotha. The way to this place is shown to him by an angel of the Lord (23.15-18). At the centre of the earth, where Adam rests, where Melchizedek officiated as priest and where Abraham went to sacrifice Isaac, there, too the cross was erected. The blood and water flowing from Christ's body baptized the protoplast (19.2-10).

In the *Cave of Treasures* the story of Adam and Eve is even more firmly embedded in a Christian retelling of the biblical story, and of the history of humanity in particular, than in the two preceding writings. These three books have a number of traditions in common and, again, it is useful to list them and to look for parallels in Jewish sources. It is interesting to note that the tradition of Adam's burial at Golgotha is already known to Origen, *Comm. ser. 126 in Matt*, and that he thinks it is of Jewish origin (for further patristic references see G.W.H. Lampe, *A Patristic Greek Lexicon*, s. v. *Adam*, section G).

If we concentrate on points of contact between the *Cave of Treasures* and the *Life of Adam and Eve*, we note again agreements with the view on the history of salvation found in the Arm.–Georg. and Lat. equivalent of *GLAE* 13.3-5, including the 5500 years, and with the story of the jealousy and fall of the devil in chs. 11–17 (Arm.-Georg. and Lat.). Next there is the dwelling of Satan in the serpent in *LAE* 16-19 and the waiting for the moment that Eve is alone (see 7.2 and 17.1-2)—for details see p. 53 above. We may add the characterization of Eve's and Adam's nudity as loss of glory in *GLAE* 20.1-2; 21.6, and the interesting detail found in *LAE* 5.3, where the Greek manuscripts A(T)LCR and Arm.-Georg. make the sons of Adam assemble 'at the door of the house where he entered to pray to God'. In the subsequent story in the *Life*, however, the fact that the farewell-meeting takes place there, is of no importance.

Again, the contact between the *Cave of Treasures* and the *Life of Adam and Eve* (in its different versions) concerns certain traditions they have in common. The claim that the *Cave of Treasures* depends directly on the *Life of Adam and Eve* cannot be substantiated. In many cases the *Cave of Treasures* departs considerably from the main themes of the *Life of Adam and Eve*. Its insistence that Adam was not punished, for instance, is totally strange to the message of the *Life*, in all its versions. Furthermore, the typological contrast between Adam and Jesus Christ, important to the view on history found in the *Cave of Treasures*, is absent from *LAE*, and it does not hint at the possibility of a contrast either. Also the stories of Adam's burial are conspicuously different.

Further Reading

E.A.W. Budge, *The Book of the Cave of Treasures* (London: Religious Tract Society, 1927).

Su-Min Ri, *La Caverne des Trésors. Les deux recensions syriaques* (CSCO; Louvain: Peeters, 1987), pp. 486-87.

The *Struggle of Adam and Eve with Satan*

The Ethiopic book with this name was translated (from one manuscript in Tübingen) by A. Dillmann in *Das christliche Adambuch des Morgenlandes* (1853). In 1882 E. Trumpp (*Der Kampf Adams*) published it, on the basis of the same manuscript and another in the British Museum, with corrections from an Arabic manuscript from Munich, which showed that the Ethiopic had been translated from an Arabic original. This text was translated into English by S.C. Malan in *The Book of Adam and Eve* (1882). On the confused nomenclature of related Syriac, Arabic and Ethiopic documents, see R.W. Cowley, *Ethiopian Biblical Interpretation* (1988), pp. 136-40.

In Arabic as well as in Ethiopic the writing often appears together with related books as part of a larger whole. As published by Trumpp it consists of three parts: 1) the struggle proper, for our present purpose the most interesting section of the book; 2) the history from Cain and Abel to Melchizedek (heavily dependent on the relevant section of the *Cave of Treasures*); and 3) a short history of the world from the death of Shem to Jesus Christ (compare again the *Cave of Treasures*). Recently an edition of the Arabic text of part 1 only was published, with an Italian translation, by A. Battista and B. Bagatti in *Il Combattimento di Adamo* (1982). It is based on nine manuscripts.

Both the Arabic and the Ethiopic versions are difficult to date. For the Ethiopic a seventh-century date has been suggested, but also the eleventh century has been mentioned. The work itself is thought to be earlier (fifth–sixth century), and it has often been assumed that it contains earlier parts, of Christian and Jewish provenance. A new edition of the Ethiopic (there are some more manuscripts) and a detailed comparison with the Arabic is needed.

In the meantime some interesting features of part 1, which tells the story of Adam and Eve in the 223 days between their expulsion from Paradise and their marriage, may be mentioned briefly. This story forms an independent unit; unlike the other two parts it does not run parallel to the corresponding part in the *Cave of Treasures*. Yet also here all events circle around this cave in the mountains near Paradise, where

Adam and Eve live, pray and fast and (later) sacrifice to the Lord. In their edition of the Arabic version Battista and Bagatti divide this story into 52 episodes, which division we shall use here.

Adam and Eve are portrayed as completely inexperienced. Having lost their garments of light and glory they have to get used to living in a body of flesh. They must learn to cope with light and darkness, heat and cold, to drink water and to eat, and to wear clothes and to make them; at the end of this story they are taught to harvest wheat and to perpetuate the human race by begetting and bearing children. All along they are helped by God, through his angels and through his word that comes to them to give the necessary explanations, instructions and encouragement. All along, too, Satan tries to seduce them and to destroy them, changing himself into an angel of light or into other creatures. Amongst other things he tries to kill Adam and Eve by lighting a fire near the cave, or hurling a large stone from the mountain, or hurting Adam with a sharp stone while he is sacrificing to God. Always the protoplasts are saved by divine intervention. God does not allow Adam and Eve to go back to Paradise and prevents their efforts to enter it, but he announces deliverance from hardship and sorrow after 5500 years, when he will himself come on earth in a human body. In helping them against Satan he shows that it is he, and not the Enemy, who is able to fulfil what he promises. Often there is a typological likeness between what happens to Adam and what the Gospels tell about Jesus Christ (so, for instance, Satan's attack with the stone makes flow blood and water from Adam's side—see Jn 19.34).

Certain traditions and motifs in the different versions of the *Life of Adam and Eve* are found here too. The period of 5500 years, mentioned repeatedly, reminds us again of the Arm.–Georg. and Lat. equivalent of Gr. 13.3-5. Also a version of the story of the fall of Satan (*LAE* 11–17 in Lat., Arm.–Georg.) recurs, this time told by angels to Adam (ep. 33). In the same episode the motif of angelic intercession for Adam is found, though not concerned with God's forgiveness after death, as in *LAE* 33–35 (Gr. and Georg., cf. Lat. 46–47), but with help for Adam to hold out until the fulfilment of God's promise. In episode 8 God forbids the wild animals to do harm to Adam and Eve (cf. Eve's and Seth's encounter with the beast in the different versions of *LAE* 10–12). This theme returns in episode 12 when the serpent into whom Satan had entered (*LAE* 16–17, this fact is also referred to elsewhere) attacks Eve again.

Another element requires attention. There are two references to the

Acherusian lake (cf. *LAE* 27.3 in Gr. and Georg.) without, however, mentioning the name. Right at the beginning of the story of the struggle with Satan there is a description of a lake with pure water, to the north of the Garden, where the bodies of the righteous and of repentant sinners will be cleansed in the last days (ep. 1). Later on Satan, again in the form of an angel, brings Adam and Eve to this lake, allegedly to purify them in view of re-entry into the Garden, in reality to throw them down from a high mountain near the lake in order to kill them. God prevents this (ep. 18). Immediately after this God gives the protoplasts gold, incense and myrrh, through his angels Michael, Gabriel and Rafael; they come out of Paradise, and serve as signs of God's covenant with Adam and Eve (ep. 19). These gifts, of course, later play an important role in parts 2 and 3 of the book, which follow the story line in the *Cave of Treasures*.

In the next episode, Adam and Eve promise to do penance for 40 days and nights. This episode obviously parallels their penance in the rivers Jordan and Tigris (*LAE* 6–10, 17 in Lat., Arm.–Georg., cf. Slav.). Satan approaches Eve in the form of an angel with the (pseudo-)message from Adam that he has received his garment of light back. She goes to Adam, who is desperate and ready to kill himself by drowning, but God prevents that. A similar interruption by Satan of a forty-day period of praying and fasting is recorded in eps. 35-38. In the thirtieth night Satan beats Adam and Eve up, and on the thirty-ninth day he seduces them by disguising himself as an angel of light. The last trick succeeds at first, but God intervenes and enables Adam and Eve to complete their fast.

It is interesting to note that elements found in versions of the *Life of Adam and Eve* are also used in the totally different, fundamentally Christian story of the *Struggle of Adam and Eve with Satan*. Although the stories might differ, certain traditions remained meaningful and popular.

Further Reading

A. Battista and B. Bagatti, *Il Combattimento di Adamo* (Jerusalem: Franciscan Printing Press, 1982).

R.W. Cowley, *Ethiopian Biblical Interpretation: A Study in Exegetical Tradition and Hermeneutics* (University of Cambridge Oriental Publications 38; Cambridge: Cambridge University Press, 1988), pp. 136-40.

A. Dillmann, *Das christliche Adambuch des Morgenlandes* (Göttingen, 1853 = *Jahrbücher der bibl. Wissenschaft* 5 [1853]), pp. 1-144.

S.C. Malan, *The Book of Adam and Eve, also called the Conflict of Adam and Eve with Satan* (London: Williams & Norgate, 1882).

E. Trumpp, 'Der Kampf Adams...oder Das christliche Adambuch des Morgenlandes,' *Abhandlungen der philos.-philol. Classe der königlich. Bayerischen Akademie der Wissenschaften* 15,3 (Munich, 1882), pp. 1-172.

The *Apocalypse of Adam*

This writing belongs to the corpus of manuscripts discovered at Nag Hammadi. It is found in Nag Hammadi Codex V, pp. 64-85. For an edition see G.W. MacRae, 'The Apocalypse of Adam, V, 5.64, 1-85, 32'. For a translation see G.W. MacRae and D.M. Parrott in J.M. Robinson (ed.), *The Nag Hammadi Library in English* (1977), and for a translation with short comments G.W. MacRae, 'Apocalypse of Adam' in J.H. Charlesworth, *OTP* I, pp. 707-19, as well as and B. Layton, 'The Revelation of Adam' in his *The Gnostic Scriptures* (1987), pp. 52-64. F. Morard has given a critical edition with commentary in her *L'Apocalypse d'Adam (NH V, 5)* (1985).

The Coptic manuscript dates from about 350. The work was composed in Greek and must be earlier, but exactly how much earlier it is, remains a matter of dispute. Because of its primitive features and its lack of distinctive elements of non-Gnostic Christianity some scholars date it in the early second century.

In the first lines the work is presented as a revelation (apocalypse) taught by Adam to Seth in the 700th year. This makes it a 'testament', for according to Gen. 5.3-5 LXX Seth was born in Adam's 230th year and Adam died 700 years later at the age of 930 (Hebrew: 130, 800 and 930 respectively). At the end (85.3-18) its contents are described as a heavenly message brought by angelic beings, and, in fact, Adam reveals to Seth what has earlier been revealed to him. Originally Adam and Eve lived in glory, like angels, and Eve taught Adam the knowledge of the Eternal God. This glory and knowledge were lost when the creator-god made them of earth, separated them, and let them serve him in fear and subjection. Their hearts were darkened. Seth, however, was called by the name of the Great Seth, whose spiritual posterity are the gnostics who are destined for salvation.

Adam's revelation is concerned with the fate of the gnostics and of the rest of humanity. Three persons, greater and more glorious than the servants of the creator-god address Adam: 'Adam! Arise from the sleep of death and hear about the eternity and the seed of That Human Being, to whom life had drawn near and which has emanated from you and from Eve your consort' (66.1-8, trans. Layton). These three persons reveal to Adam what will happen.

First there is the Flood, caused by the creator-god to destroy humanity including the gnostics whom he regards as a menace. After the Flood he makes a covenant with Noah (called Deucalion) and Noah divides the whole land between his sons Ham, Japheth and Shem. Again, however, people 'called by that Name (of Seth)' appear, 'they dwell there six hundred years in acquaintance with incorruptibility' (72.6-9). Four hundred thousand people belonging to the posterity of Ham and Japheth will join them; the rest of the Hamides and Japhetides will form twelve kingdoms. The creator intervenes with a storm of fire, brimstone and asphalt, but heavenly powers rescue the true gnostics from fire and wrath.

Again, for a third time, 'the luminary of acquaintance will pass by in great glory' (76.8-11) so that they who reflect upon the knowledge of the Eternal God will not perish. He will perform many signs and wonders and the creator is greatly perturbed because of this Man's superiority. He raises up great wrath against him. 'And the glory shall go elsewhere and dwell in holy buildings that it has chosen for itself. And the powers will not see it with their own eyes, nor will they see the other luminary. Next, they will chastise the flesh of that human being upon whom the holy Spirit has come' (77.9-18).

Those who are not enlightened by the true knowledge cannot understand the 'luminary' sent by the Eternal God. This is illustrated by a summing-up of the (mis)interpretations of his appearance by the twelve kingdoms. A thirteenth kingdom (the four hundred thousand from Ham and Japheth?) speak of a Word that received glory and power, the race 'without a king over it', the true gnostics, recognize him as chosen by God from all the aeons. The book ends with a glorification of the posterity of Seth, and with a lament of the others who realize their folly and transgression resulting in the death of their souls. Unexpectedly an invective against proponents of (an improper sort of) baptism follows.

The interpretation of this apocalypse presents many difficulties, which need not detain us here; to assess it properly one has to study it in the context of Sethian gnosticism. The Genesis stories of Adam and Eve and of the Flood are presupposed, but have no more than a background function. The place of Satan in other stories about Adam and Eve is played by the creator-god, and the central problem of humanity is lack of spiritual insight rather than sin and guilt. Salvation means incorruptibility, destined for those who have received insight into the truth of the Supreme God. Seth, the human son of Adam and Eve, receives this revelation but seems to play no part in the subsequent history of humanity—determined by the heavenly Seth as far as the true gnostics are concerned. Noah and his sons, including Shem, belong to the world of the creator-god, except the four hundred thousand from Ham and Japheth (whose position, however, remains somewhat shadowy).

It does not come as a surprise that there are hardly any points of contact between the *Apocalypse of Adam* and the primary and secondary Adam books discussed earlier. In his contribution 'Some Related Traditions in the Apocalypse of Adam, the Books of Adam and Eve and 1 Enoch' (1981), G.W.E. Nickelsburg has suggested by way of hypothesis: 'Both *Adam and Eve* 29.2-10, 49-50 and the apocalypse in *ApocAd* stem from a common tradition, an apocalyptic testament of Adam which was influenced by the Apocalypse of Weeks and perhaps other Enochic traditions' (p. 537). It would seem that, given the nature of the evidence, this has to remain hypothetical.

Furthermore, we should note that both *LAE*-passages mentioned have been taken from the Latin version, and that 29.3-10 is not found in the manuscripts belonging to Meyer's family I (see Chapter 1, p. 14). As to Eve's farewell speech in *LLAE* 49–50: Her command to Seth to write the story of the protoplasts on tablets of stone and clay so that they may survive the coming judgments with water and fire, has been connected (also by others than Nickelsburg) with the interventions by the creator-god, first at the Flood and next with fire (cf. Gen. 19.24-25) in the *Apocalypse of Adam*, as well as with the enigmatic statements at the end of this apocalypse about the revelations by the angelic beings. We hear that they 'have not been inscribed in (the form of a) book nor are they in writing'; at the same time 'they will be situated atop a high mountain upon a rock of truth' (85.6-11). This connection seems very tenuous; it should be noted also that an injunction by Adam to Seth similar to that found in *LLAE* 49–50 is recorded by Josephus in *Antiquities* 1.2.67-71.

Further Reading

B. Layton, 'The Revelation of Adam' in his *The Gnostic Scriptures* (Garden City, NY: Doubleday, 1987), pp. 52-64.

G.W. MacRae and D.M. Parrott in J.M. Robinson (ed.), *The Nag Hammadi Library in English* (Leiden: Brill, 1977), pp 256-64.

G.W. MacRae, 'Apocalypse of Adam' in J.H. Charlesworth, *The Old Testament Pseudepigrapha* (Garden City, NY: Doubleday, 1981), I, pp. 707-19.

—'The Apocalypse of Adam, V, 5: 64, 1-85, 32' in D.M. Parrott (ed.), *Nag Hammadi Codices V, 2-5 and VI with Papyrus Berolinensis 8502,1 and 4* (The Coptic Gnostic Library, NHS 11; Leiden: Brill, 1979), pp. 151-95.

F. Morard, *L'Apocalypse d'Adam* (*NH V*, 5) (Bibl. Copte de Nag Hammadi, Textes 15; Québec: Presses de l'Université Laval, 1985).

G.W.E. Nickelsburg, 'Some Related Traditions in the Apocalypse of Adam, the Books of Adam and Eve and 1 Enoch' in B. Layton (ed.), *The Rediscovery of Gnosticism; vol. 2 Sethian Gnosticism* (Suppl. to *Numen* 41, 2; Leiden: Brill, 1981), pp. 515-39.

Conclusions

Stories about Adam and Eve remained important in the early Church (and later); a number of traditions which are found in the different versions of the *Life of Adam and Eve* also made their way into a number of Adam documents of later times. Literary dependence of the latter on one or more versions of the *Life* cannot be proved, but it cannot be excluded that knowledge of (a) version(s) of the *Life* stimulated some authors to take up particular traditions, and to insert them into their own writings. At the same time the popularity of these traditions may have contributed to the fact that the *Life of Adam and Eve* continued to be handed down to further generations, either by simply copying it, and/or by expansion of its contents by adding new features, or by translation into other languages used by Christians.

Select Bibliography

Adler, W., *Time Immemorial: Archaic History and its Sources in Christian Chronography from Julius Africanus to George Syncellus* (Dumbarton Oaks Studies, 26; Washington: Dumbarton Oaks, 1989).

Anderson, G.A., 'Celibacy or Consummation in the Garden? Reflections on Early Jewish and Christian Interpretations of the Garden of Eden', *HTR* 82 (1989), pp. 121-48.

—'The Penitence Narrative in the Life of Adam and Eve', *HUCA* 63 (1992), pp. 1-39.

Anderson, G.A., and M.E. Stone, *A Synopsis of the Books of Adam and Eve* (SBL Early Judaism and its Literature, 5; Atlanta: Scholars Press, 1994).

Battista, A., and B. Bagatti, *Il Combattimento di Adamo* (Jerusalem: Franciscan Printing Press, 1982).

Bertrand, D.A.., 'Le destin "post mortem" des protoplastes selon la "Vie grecque d'Adam et Eve"', in *La littérature intertestamentaire: Colloque de Strasbourg (17–19 Octobre 1983)* (Paris: Presses Universitaires de France, 1985), pp. 109-18

—*La vie grecque d'Adam et Eve* (Recherches intertestamentaires, 1; Paris: Maisonneuve, 1987).

—in A. Dupont-Sommer and M. Philonenko (eds.), *La Bible, Ecrits Intertestamentaires* (Paris: Gallimard, 1987), pp. 1765-96.

Bianchi, U., 'La rédemption dans les livres d'Adam', *Numen* 18 (1971), pp. 1-8.

Brock, S.P., 'Jewish Traditions in Syriac Sources', *JJS* 30 (1979), pp. 212-32.

Budge, E.A.W., 'The Discourse on Abbatôn', in idem, *Coptic Martyrdoms etc. in the Dialect of Upper Egypt* (London: British Museum, 1914), pp., x-xi; xxii-xxiii; lxviii-lxxii (introductions and summary), pp. 225-49 (text) and pp. 482-91 (translation).

—*The Book of the Cave of Treasures* (London: Religious Tract Society, 1927).

Burmester, O.H.E., 'Egyptian Mythology in the Coptic Apocrypha', *Orientalia* 7 (1938), pp. 355-67.

—*Koptische Handschriften. I. Die Handschriftenfragmente der Staats- und Universitätsbibliothek Hamburg* (VOHD, 21.1; Wiesbaden: Steiner, 1975), Suppl. 26, p. 305.

Ceriani, A.-M., in 'Apocalypsis Moysi in medio mutila', in *Monumenta Sacra et Profana. V.2. Opuscula et fragmenta miscella magnam partem apocrypha* (Milan: Bibliotheca Ambrosiana, 1868), pp. 19-24.

Cortès, E., *Los discursos de adiós des Gn 49 a Jn 13–17: Pistas para la historia de un género literario en la antigua judía* (Barcelona: Herder, 1976).

Cowley, R.W., *Ethiopian Biblical Interpretation: A Study in Exegetical Tradition and Hermeneutics* (University of Cambridge Oriental Publications, 38; Cambridge: Cambridge University Press, 1988), pp. 136-40.

Crum, W.E., *Catalogue of Coptic Manuscripts in the Collection of the John Rylands Library* (Manchester: Manchester University Press, 1909), p. 40 n. 84.

Denis, A.-M., *Introduction aux pseudépigraphes grecs d'Ancien Testament* (SVTP, 1; Leiden: Brill, 1970), pp. 3-14.

Dillmann, A., *Das christliche Adambuch des Morgenlandes* (Göttingen, 1853 = *Jahrbücher der bibl. Wissenschaft* 5 [1853], pp. 1-144).

Dobschütz, E. von, *Das Decretum Gelasianum de libris recipiendis et non recipiendis* (Texte und Untersuchungen, 38.4; Leipzig: Hinrichs, 1912).

Elliott, J.K., *The Apocryphal New Testament* (Oxford: Clarendon Press, 1993).

Fehrenbach, E., 'Encens', in, *Dictionnaire d'archéologie chrétienne et de liturgie* V.1 (Paris: Letouzey, 1922), cols. 2-21.

Fernández Marcos, N., in A. Díez Macho, *Apócrifos del Antiguo Testamento* (Madrid: Ediciones Cristiandad, 1983), II, pp. 317-52.

Frey, J.-B., 'Adam (Livres apocryphes sous son nom)', in *Dictionnaire de la Bible: Supplément* (Paris: Letouzey et Ané, 1928), I, pp. 101-134.

Fuchs, C., in E. Kautzsch, *Die Apokryphen und Pseudepigraphen des Alten Testaments* (Tübingen 1900; repr. Darmstadt: Wissenschaftliche Buchgesellschaft, 1962), pp. 506-28.

Gelzer, H., *Sextus Julius Africanus und die byzantinische Chronologie* II (Leipzig: Hinrichs, 1885).

Ginzberg, L., *The Legends of the Jews* (7 vols.; Philadelphia: Jewish Publication Society of America, 1909–38).

Halford, M.B., 'The Apocryphal Vita Adae et Evae: Some Comments on the Manuscript Tradition', *Neuphilologische Mitteilungen* 82 (1981), pp. 417-27.

Hollander, H.W., 'The Testaments of the Twelve Patriarchs', in M. de Jonge (ed.), *Outside the Old Testament* (Cambridge: Cambridge University Press, 1985), pp. 71-91.

Janson, A.G.P., and L.R.A. Van Rompay, *Efrem de Syriër. Uitleg van het boek Genesis* (Kampen: Kok, 1993).

Jagić, V., 'Slavische Beiträge zu den biblischen Apocryphen, I, Die altkirchenslavischen Texte des Adambuches', *Denkschriften der kaiserlichen Akademie der Wissenschaften* (Phil. Hist. Classe, 42.1; Vienna, 1893), pp. 1-104.

Johnson, M.D., in J.H. Charlesworth (ed.), *The Old Testament Pseudepigrapha* (Garden City, NY: Doubleday, 1983–85), II, pp. 249-95.

Kaestli, J.D., and P. Cherix, *L'évangile de Barthélémy d'après deux écrits apocryphes* (Turnhout: Brepols, 1993).

Kolenkow, A.B., 'Trips to the Other World in Antiquity and the Story of Seth in the Life of Adam and Eve', in P.J. Achtemeier (ed.) (SBLSP; Missoula, MT: Scholars Press, 1977), pp. 1-11.

K'urc'idze, C'., 'Adamis apokrip'uli c'xovrebis k'art'uli versia', *P'ilologiuri dziebani* 1 (1964), pp. 97-136.

Layton, B., 'The Revelation of Adam' in his *The Gnostic Scriptures* (Garden City, NY: Doubleday, 1987), pp. 52-64.

Lampe, G.W.H., *A Patristic Greek Lexicon* (Oxford: Clarendon Press, 1961).

Leipoldt, J., *Ägyptische Urkunden aus den königlichen Museen zu Berlin* (Berlin: Weidmann, 1904), I, pp. 171-172 n. 181.

Levison, J.R., 'The Exoneration of Eve in the Apocalypse of Moses', *JSJ* 20 (1989), pp. 135-50.

—*Portraits of Adam in Early Judaism from Sirach to 2 Baruch* (JSPSup, 1; Sheffield: JSOT Press, 1988).

Lipscomb, W.L., *The Armenian Apocryphal Adam Literature* (University of Pennsylvania Armenian Texts and Studies, 8; Pittsburgh: University of Pennsylvania Press, 1990).

MacRae, G.W., and D.M. Parrott, in J.M. Robinson (ed.), *The Nag Hammadi Library in English* (Leiden: Brill, 1977), pp. 256-64.

MacRae, G.W., 'Apocalypse of Adam' in J.H. Charlesworth, *The Old Testament Pseudepigrapha* (Garden City, NY: Doubleday, 1981), I, pp. 707-19.

—'The Apocalypse of Adam, V,5 : 64,1-85, 32', in D.M. Parrott (ed.), *Nag Hammadi Codices V, 2-5 and VI with Papyrus Berolinensis 8502,1 and 4* (The Coptic Gnostic Library, NHS 11; Leiden: Brill, 1979), pp. 151-95.

Mahé, J.-P., 'Le livre d'Adam géorgien', in R. van den Broek and M.J. Vermaseren (eds.), *Studies in Gnosticism and Hellenistic religions* (Feschrift G. Quispel; EPROER, 91; Leiden: Brill, 1981), pp. 227-60.

—'Notes philologiques sur la version géorgienne de la Vita Adae', *Bedi Kartlisa, Revue de Kartvélologie* 41 (1983), pp. 51-66.

Malan, S.C., *The Book of Adam and Eve, also called the Conflict of Adam and Eve with Satan* (London: Williams & Norgate, 1882).

Metzger, M. (ed.), *Les constitutions apostoliques* II (Sources chrétiennes 329; Paris: Cerf, 1986).

Meyer, W., 'Vita Adae et Evae', *Abhandlungen der philosophisch-philologischen Klasse der königlichen Bayerischen Akademie der Wissenschaften* 14.3 (Munich, 1878), pp. 185-250.

Mosshammer, A.A. (ed.), *Georgius Syncellus: Ecloga chronographica* (Leipzig: Teubner, 1984).

Morard, F., *L'Apocalypse d'Adam (NH V, 5)* (Bibl. Copte de Nag Hammadi, Textes 15; Québec: Presses de l'Université Laval, 1985).

Mozley, J.H., 'The 'Vita Adae'', JTS 30 (1929), pp. 121-47.

Müller, C.D.G., *Die Engellehre der Koptischen Kirche* (Wiesbaden: Harrassowitz,1959).

Nagel, M., *La vie d'Adam et d'Eve* (Apocalypse de Moïse) I-III (Lille: Service de Réproduction des Thèses, 1974) .

—preliminary edition in A.-M. Denis O.P., *Concordance grecque des pseudépigraphes d'Ancien Testament* (Louvain-la-Neuve: Brepols, 1987), pp. 815-18.

Nickelsburg, G.W.E., in M.E. Stone (ed.), *Jewish Writings of the Second Temple Period* (CRINT, 2.2; Assen/Philadelphia: Van Gorcum/Fortress, 1984), pp. 110-18.

—'Some Related Traditions in the Apocalypse of Adam, the Books of Adam and Eve and 1 Enoch' in B. Layton (ed.), *The Rediscovery of Gnosticism*. II. *Sethian Gnosticism* (Suppl. to Numen 41.2; Leiden: Brill, 1981), pp. 515-39.

Nordheim, E. von, *Die Lehre der Alten* I-II (Leiden: Brill, 1980–85).

Peterson, E., 'Die "Taufe" im Acherusischen See', *VC* 9 (1955), pp. 1-20 = *idem, Frühkirche, Judentum und Gnosis* (Rome–Freiburg–Vienna: Herder, 1959), pp. 310-32.

Piñero, A., 'Angels and Demons in the Greek Life of Adam and Eve', *JSJ* 24 (1993), pp. 191-214.

Poorthuis, M., 'Sexisme als zondeval. Rabbijnse interpretaties van het paradijsverhaal belicht vanuit de verhouding tussen man en vrouw', *Tijdschrift voor Theologie* 30 (1990), pp. 234-58.

Quinn, E.C., *The Quest of Seth for the Oil of Life* (Chicago: University of Chicago Press, 1962).

Riessler, P., *Altjüdisches Schrifttum ausserhalb der Bibel* (Heidelberg, 1928; repr. Darmstadt: Wissenschaftliche Buchgesellschaft, 1966), pp. 138-55, 668-881.

Robinson, S.E., 'Testament of Adam', in J.H. Charlesworth, *The Old Testament Pseudepigrapha* (Garden City, NY: Doubleday, 1983), I, pp. 989-95.

—*The Testament of Adam* (SBLDS, 52; Chico, CA: Scholars Press, 1982).

Scheidweiler, F., 'Nikodemusevangelium, Pilatusakten und Höllenfahrt Christi' in W. Schneemelcher, *Neutestamentliche Apokryphen* (Tübingen: Mohr, 5th edn, 1989), I, pp. 395-424.

Schürer, E., *The History of the Jewish People in the Age of Jesus Christ (175 B.C.–A.D. 135).* A New English Version revised and edited by G. Vermes, F. Millar and M. Goodman, III.2 (Edinburgh: T. & T. Clark, 1987), pp. 757-61.

Sharpe, J.L., *Prolegomena to the Establishment of the Critical Text of the Greek Apocalypse of Moses* (unpublished PhD dissertation, Duke University, 1969).

Sparks, H.F.D. (ed.), *The Apocryphal Old Testament* (Oxford: Clarendon Press, 1984).

Stone, M.E., *The Penitence of Adam* (CSCO, 429–30; Louvain: Peeters, 1981).

—*Armenian Apocrypha relating to the Patriarchs and Prophets* (Jerusalem: Israel Academy of Sciences and Humanities, 1982), pp. 39-51.

—*A History of the Literature of Adam and Eve* (SBL Early Judaism and its Literature, 3; Atlanta: Scholars Press, 1992).

—'The Fall of Satan and Adam's Penance; Three notes on the Books of Adam and Eve', *JTS* NS 44 (1993), pp. 143-56.

—*Armenian Apocrypha Relating to Adam and Eve* (SVTP, 14; Leiden: Brill, 1996).

Su-Min Ri, *La Caverne des Trésors. Les deux recensions syriaques* (CSCO, 486–87; Louvain: Peeters, 1987).

Sweet, A.M., *A Religio-Historical Study of the Greek Life of Adam and Eve* (unpublished PhD dissertation, Notre Dame, 1992).

Tischendorf, C., *Apocalypses Apocryphae* (Leipzig, 1866; repr. Hildesheim: Olms, 1966), pp. 1-23.

—'Ὑπομνήματα τοῦ κυρίου ἡμῶν Ἰησοῦ Χριστοῦ πραχθέντα ἐπὶ Πόντιου Πιλάτου; Gesta Pilati; Evangelii Nicodemi pars altera sive Descensus Christi ad inferos', in *Evangelia apocrypha* (Leipzig, 2nd edn, 1876; repr. Hildesheim: Olms, 1966), pp. 210-432.

Tonneau, R.-M. (ed.), *Sancti Ephraem Syri in Genesim et in Exodum commentarii* (CSCO, 152; Louvain: Peeters, 1955).

Tromp, J., *The Assumption of Moses: A Critical Edition with Commentary* (SVTP, 10; Leiden: Brill, 1993).

—'Literary and Exegetical Issues in the Story of Adam's Death and Burial (*GLAE* 31–42)', in J. Frishman and L. Van Rompay (eds.), *The Book of Genesis in Jewish and Oriental Christian Interpretation* (Traditio Exegetica Graeca, 5; Louvain: Peeters, 1997).

Trumpp, E., 'Der Kampf Adams... oder Das christliche Adambuch des Morgenlandes', in *Abhandlungen der philos.-philol. Classe der königlich. Bayerischen Akademie der Wissenschaften* XV.3 (Munich, 1882), pp. 1-172.

Turdeanu, E., 'La Vie d'Adam et d'Eve en slave et en roumain', in *Apocryphes slaves et roumains de l'Ancien Testament* (SVTP, 5; Leiden: Brill, 1981), pp. 75-144 and 437-38.

Wells, L.S.A. in R.H. Charles (ed.), *The Apocrypha and Pseudepigrapha of the Old Testament* (Oxford: Clarendon Press, 1913), II, pp. 123-54.

Whittaker, M., 'The Life of Adam and Eve', in H.F.D. Sparks (ed.), *The Apocryphal Old Testament* (Oxford: Clarendon Press, 1984), pp. 141-67.

Zahn, T., *Geschichte des neutestamentlichen Kanons*, II.1 (Erlangen/ Leipzig: Deichert, 1890).

For further bibliographical details see M.E. Stone, *A History of the Literature of Adam and Eve*, pp. 125-53.

INDEXES

INDEX OF REFERENCES

BIBLE

INDEX OF AUTHORS